Makers of the Modern Theological Mind

Bob E. Patterson, Editor

Makers of the Modern Theological Mind

Bob E. Patterson, Editor

H. RICHARD NIEBUHR

by Lonnie D. Kliever

Word Books, Publisher, Waco, Texas

H. Richard Niebuhr

ISBN 0-8499-0078-6
Library of Congress catalog card number: 77–92452
Printed in the United States of America

For Launa and Marney

Contents

Editor's Preface

Who are the thinkers that have shaped Christian theology in our time? This series tries to answer that question by providing a reliable guide to the ideas of the men who have significantly charted the theological seas of our century. In the current revival of theology, these books will give a new generation the opportunity to be exposed to significant minds. They are not meant, however, to be a substitute for a careful study of the original works of these makers of the modern theological mind.

This series is not for the lazy. Each major theologian is examined carefully and critically—his life, his theological method, his most germinal ideas, his weaknesses as a thinker, his place in the theological spectrum, and his chief contribution to the climate of theology today. The books are written with the assumption that laymen will read them and enter into the theological dialogue that is so necessary to the church as a whole. At the same time they are carefully enough designed to give assurance to a Ph.D. student in theology preparing for his preliminary exams.

Each author in the series is a professional scholar and theologian in his own right. All are specialists on, and in some cases have studied with, the theologians about whom they write. Welcome to the series.

Bob E. Patterson, Editor
Baylor University

Preface

Writing this book has been a special joy for two reasons. First, it lets me introduce the readers of this series to one of the great "makers of the modern theological mind." H. Richard Niebuhr is less prolific in his writings than others of his theological generation, but his seven slim volumes and half a hundred articles have earned him a permanent place in the history of Christian thought. He has contributed seminal studies in the sociology and philosophy of religion as well as ground-breaking work in theology, ethics and American religious history. Most important of all, he has fashioned a creative synthesis of radical monotheism and cultural pluralism that illumines the perennial hopes of mankind and the special problems of our time. Second, writing this book lets me publicly acknowledge appreciation for my greatest teacher. Though we never met and exchanged letters but once, H. Richard Niebuhr entered my life and mind as the subject for my doctoral dissertation fifteen years ago at Duke University. For reasons both broadly cultural and intensely personal, I have been unable to go his way theologically. But he has taught me so much through his writings that he remains a permanent companion in the human quest for meaningful existence in our time.

There are several people who deserve recognition and gratitude for their contributions to this study. I am indebted to the general editor of this series, Dr. Bob E. Patterson, for persisting over several years to ask that I lay aside research more urgent to my personal concerns to do the Niebuhr book for the series. The "distraction" has fueled my thinking in unexpected and important ways. Gloria W. Green and Ruth I. Kimler deserve credit for turning my working drafts into a finished typescript. The many suggestions of my wife Arthiss considerably improved the prose and clarified the thought in the final drafting. My good friend Martin Rumscheidt read the finished manuscript with a fine eye for accuracy and consistency. Finally, I wish to thank two persons who contributed the humanizing distractions that every author needs to remember that life is more than books—my daughters Launa Deane and Marney Marie Kliever. To them this book is dedicated.

LONNIE D. KLIEVER

Part One

NIEBUHR AS REFORMER

I. Niebuhr's Life

THE LEGACY OF REFORMATION

Looking back over thirty years of his life, H. Richard Niebuhr acknowledged a continuous and continuing imperative in his own Christian life and work: "I still believe that reformation is a permanent movement, that *metanoia* is the continuous demand made upon us in historical life." [1] Thus his own shifts in theological emphasis, alterations in moral counsel, and changes in ecclesiastical strategy over the years were and are in service to the renewal of church and society at a particular historical time and place. The Christian and the church are not called to be unswerving in doctrinal, ethical or ecclesiastical position. Rather they are always and only to be centered on what God is doing and requiring in concrete cases and circumstances. Precisely this demand, according to Niebuhr, is why the reformation of theology and ethics is the unending pilgrimage of the Christian life and the unending vocation of the Christian theologian.

In the years since his death in 1962, Niebuhr has more and more been acclaimed as *the* twentieth-century reformer among North American theologians. [2] Apart from the excellence of his work, this acclaim reflects two features of the contemporary theological scene in this country. On the one hand, there are no clear and commanding theological luminaries leading the way for our generation. But those who are doing theology today remember when there *were* "giants in the land"—Reinhold Niebuhr, Paul Tillich, H. Richard Niebuhr—who reshaped the religious consciousness of North American culture. On the other hand, recent theological and religious studies have become increasingly aware of theology's cultural roots and reflections. This new attention to *American* religion and *American* theology has spotlighted our indigenous theologians—those thinkers who have newly translated historic Christianity and European influences into native symbolic forms and cultural preoccupations. In this regard, the Niebuhr brothers stand out among American theologians of this century. Each has wrought a highly original and influential reformation of the Christian message and life of faith for our time. Comparisons between the two are as difficult as they are inevitable. Their theologies are as different as the musical instruments they played as boys in the family ensemble —Reinhold the trombone and Richard the flute. The older Niebuhr's thought is bold, chastening, somber; that of the younger is intricate, wooing, lyrical. But at the present time it does not seem exaggerated to claim that H. Richard Niebuhr's contribution to the ongoing reformation of the church and society in North America equals if not surpasses any other twentieth-century figure including his brother.

Speaking of Niebuhr in this way would not only embarrass him personally but trouble him theologically were he still alive. The last thing that he would have wanted was for *his* theology to become the focus for the reformation of religion and society. Indeed, the negative side of his own contribution to reform is directed against absolutizing *any* embodiment or concretion of faith. Niebuhr profoundly believed that "self-defensiveness" is the most prevalent source of all error and evil. Christian theology and ethics can and must bear witness to God from the standpoint of its own particular community with its particular symbols. But such a "confessional" approach permits *no* claims for the superiority and exclusivism of Christianity. No theology or ethics—be it ever so ecumenical and apostolic—furnishes the norms or the content of that perpetual revolution of personal and social existence called "faith." For Niebuhr, the focus of reformation is *God*—God with us as each moment's Creator, Judge and Redeemer.

But precisely this critique of all claims to finality and completion is what makes Niebuhr an exemplary reformer. His thinking and writing reflect a deliberate search for the growing edges of meaning beyond all existing formulation. To be sure, this search was not an exercise of introspection in isolation from the experiences and writings of others. Niebuhr fashioned his personal and vocational response to God in conversation with a wide community among the living and the dead. He listened and learned from all the voices that speak to the human condition whether their grammar was orthodox or heretical, biblical or secular, systematic or dramatic. But each voice was critically heard as a witness, more or less faithful, to the One God whose reign is without escape and whose commonwealth is without end. Thus, because the style and substance of his thought remains centered on the Absolute beyond the relative, Niebuhr might well be a reformer for all seasons. He calls us to seek the fuller truth about ourselves and our universe in and through but always beyond our highest revelations and noblest achievements.

This call was for Niebuhr fully consistent with and demanded by Christianity's revelations and achievements. The God revealed in Jesus Christ and mediated through Christian history is no "Christian"—especially no White Anglo-Saxon Protestant Patron. God is the Death-Dealer and Life-Giver, moving through all events without favoritism or capriciousness. For Niebuhr, being a Christian means teasing out the tragedy and grace at the heart of reality through a paradigm given in Christian history but not limited to Christian experience—a paradigm of crucifixion-and-resurrection. That paradigm deciphers life as "permanent revolution," as the breaking down and building up of a community that is not identical with any of the communities of this world, even democratic or Christian communities. Being a Christian means responding to that process as the action of the One God on us all.

Niebuhr's widened and widening interpretation of Christian faith was deeply rooted in his personal life and is reflected in his developed authorship. In his life and writings Christian understanding and practice became increasingly less restricted to the church through the years. For Niebuhr, this did not mean putting other groups and their traditions above the church and its scriptures. But it did mean placing them alongside as causes for concern and as resources for understanding. More important, it meant seeing all such communities and constructions as expressions of faith and as summoned to a permanent movement of reformation. A full accounting of this interpretation of Christian understanding and practice must await the following discussion on Niebuhr's theology and ethics. But a preliminary survey of his life and development here will underwrite the confessional and continuing character of his reformation of the message and life of faith in the One God.

PREPARATION FOR MINISTRY

Despite his acknowledgment that the theologian's formulations of faith are most profoundly affected by his own personal experiences, Niebuhr remained silent about those influences in his classroom lectures and published writings. He believed that he owed acknowledgment of them, insofar as they could be recognized, only to God and to himself.[3] Out of respect for that reticence, family and intimates have also remained guarded since his death about the autobiographical roots of his thought. But several recent studies drawing on unpublished materials from Niebuhr's files and on the personal recollections of family and friends have begun to trace the connections between his life-story and his theological scholarship.[4] These connections are neither spectacular nor surprising since they were there to be seen all the while in the distinctive passion and problematics that lie at the heart of his thought. Thus an introductory biographical sketch will furnish the human context and offer some important clues for the subsequent analysis of Niebuhr's thought.

The circumstances of Niebuhr's birth are symbolic of his career and contribution as a reformer of American religion and society. Born in the manse of German-American parents, he joined the cultural heritage of Germany with the social pragmatism of America in a creative blending of perspectives and preoccupations. More particularly, he combined unaffected piety and stringent learning, theological liberality and evangelical sobriety, priestly care and prophetic critique in a ministry and scholarship distinctively biblical yet modern, protestant yet ecumenical, American yet global.

Helmut Richard Niebuhr was born on September 3, 1894, in Wright City, Missouri, to Gustav and Lydia Niebuhr. He was the youngest of four surviving children that included one sister, Hulda, who was for many years professor of Christian education at McCormick Theological Seminary in Chicago, and a brother, Reinhold, two years his senior, who led the twentieth-century revival of American theology for many years as professor of applied Christianity at Union Theological Seminary in New York. Richard's father, who had immigrated to the United States from Germany at the age of seventeen, was a distinguished minister in the German Evangelical Synod of North America. His mother was the daughter of a German-American pastor under whom Gustav served during his early ministry. In this bilingual home, music, art, literature and theology were weekly fare. The children were daily treated to readings from the Bible in Hebrew and Greek, and early on were introduced to German liberal theology through the writings of Adolf von Harnack.

Given these beginnings, Richard's decision to follow his father and brother into the ministry of the German Evangelical Church is not surprising. He enrolled in his denomination's college, Elmhurst College near Chicago, in 1908 and received the Bachelor of Arts in 1912. Retracing his father's and brother's footsteps, he studied for three years at Eden Theological Seminary near St. Louis. During this time his father died (1913), and his mother returned to Lincoln, Illinois, where his father had previously served a church. After graduation from Eden in 1915, Richard also returned to Lincoln where he lived for a year and worked for a time on the staff of a daily newspaper. During that time, while attending his father's former church, he met Florence Marie Mittendorf. They were married in 1920 and in later years had two children. His son, Richard Reinhold, now continues the Niebuhr heritage, serving as a distinguished theologian at the Harvard Divinity School.

In 1916 Niebuhr was ordained and called to the Walnut Park Evangelical Church in St. Louis. Members of the church remember him as a highly committed, energetic and scholarly pastor. They also recall a tragic accident that deeply affected their young minister. While on a winter camping trip with a group of young people from the church, two brothers fell through thin ice and drowned despite Niebuhr's repeated efforts to save them. The memory of that tragedy may have contributed to his lifelong struggle with the inscrutable evil in life and with the complicity of both God and man in that evil.

Niebuhr's bent for scholarship was evidently not fully satisfied in the parish ministry. During his tenure at Walnut Park, he completed a master's degree in history at Washington University in St. Louis in two years. In 1919 he was invited to return to Eden Theological Seminary as a teacher of theology and ethics. He accepted the offer and served for three years on the faculty. These were exceedingly busy years, given the beginning professor's inevitable scramble to prepare lectures and the new groom's devoted attention to home life. Moreover, he managed a summer of study at the University of Chicago in 1921. This summer sabbatical was of lasting importance, since it was probably then that he encountered George Herbert Mead, whose social philosophy and psychology exerted a permanent influence on his thinking.

Niebuhr resumed formal theological studies full-time at Yale Divinity School in 1922. Although serving a Congregational church as pastor in nearby Clinton, Connecticut, he earned both a B.D. and a Ph.D. by 1924. His most important teachers during these years were Professors Frank C. Porter and D. C. Macintosh. The latter was especially crucial, since he directed Niebuhr's doctoral dissertation on "Ernst Troeltsch's Philosophy of Religion," and he exemplified a new way of doing theology centered in values. Niebuhr's emergence during the next decade as a new theological voice on the American scene grew largely out of a creative reinterpretation of the value methods represented by Macintosh and the historical relativism exemplified by Troeltsch. Indeed, the difficult necessity of placing human value and historical relativism at the center of theological work became a permanent feature and continuing agenda in Niebuhr's reflection.

TEACHER OF CHURCHMEN

Niebuhr was invited to remain at Yale to take over some of Professor Porter's courses in New Testament theology. He chose instead to become president of Elmhurst College. Under Niebuhr's leadership the small college made significant strides financially and academically, including the achievement of full accreditation. But once again the distractions from scholarship by other duties proved too great and Niebuhr welcomed an invitation to return to teaching at Eden Theological Seminary in 1927. He spent four productive years there, including the publication of his first book, *The Social Sources of Denominationalism* (1929).[5] This trenchant historical and sociological study of Christianity turned Niebuhr directly to the task of developing an adequate theological basis for church reform. It also set a pattern for the way Niebuhr would approach theological work —careful analysis of the historical development and alternative formulations of the issues, followed by his own attempt at synthesis.

A sabbatical leave spent in Germany in 1930 confirmed for Niebuhr the way that task had been taking shape. Already he was deeply involved in a critical and dialectical juxtaposition of nineteenth- and twentieth-century German theology with the American social gospel. He was convinced that German and

American Christianity needed a "third piece" to unite their strengths and obviate their weaknesses.[6] But the many professors and places he visited in Germany, along with a side trip to Russia, brought new urgency and focus to his search for a mediating way. Dominant among these influences was the prophetic power of two theologians among the "German Realists"—Karl Barth and especially Paul Tillich. The latter Niebuhr introduced to English readers shortly after his return to the United States by translating Tillich's *The Religious Situation* (1932).[7] Less lasting in influence but important nonetheless were Niebuhr's impressions of the social power of Marxism as a practical faith. In later years he would often allude to the example of Marxism in calling for the church to ground her strategies of reform in a practical philosophy of history.

These new influences were to be followed out in yet another change of setting. Returning from Europe, Niebuhr and his wife were still on board ship in New York Harbor when a letter was brought on board offering him an appointment as associate professor of Christian ethics at the Yale Divinity School. Niebuhr deferred the decision for a year, reluctant to give up the deep ties of place and work that his family had found at Eden. He finally did accept Yale's invitation, and the Niebuhrs moved to New Haven in time to begin the fall semester in 1931.

During the next ten years Niebuhr worked out the essential form and content of his theological synthesis and ethical stance. This labor was not, however, achieved in ivory-towered isolation from the ongoing life of the church and the world. Niebuhr's mediating position was forged in the heat of a world shaken by the rumblings of war, a nation mired in economic depression, and a church entangled in social evils. His practical concerns are obvious from the list of journal articles published during this time—for example, "Faith, Works and Social Salvation," "Nationalism, Socialism and Christianity," "Toward the Emancipation of the Church," "The Attack upon the Social Gospel," "The Christian Evangel and Social Culture." [8] This same thinking *in situ* is reflected in three important books from this same period. In a book entitled *The Church Against the World*

(1935),[9] coauthored with Wilhelm Pauck and Francis P. Miller, Niebuhr scored the church's uncritical alliances with capitalism, nationalism and humanism. Against such alliances he counseled a strategic withdrawal of the church from the world. In a more measured and scholarly work, *The Kingdom of God in America* (1937),[10] Niebuhr traced the central theme uniting American religious history as a way of testing his theological and ethical ideas in the laboratory of history and of understanding the present-day problems of American Protestantism. Finally, Niebuhr's search for a mediating way to do theology reached full fruition in *The Meaning of Revelation* (1941),[11] a timely manifesto for the continuing reformation of religion and society. For Niebuhr, responsible theology is responsive theology, responsive to God but always to God in a particular situation. Even Niebuhr's more refined and abstract thinking reflects and redirects concrete sociohistorical situations.

The international situation worsened into World War II, during which time Niebuhr wrote several probing and poignant articles dealing with war as "crucifixion"—as the redemptive suffering of both God and man.[12] So deep and difficult were Niebuhr's struggles to shape a Christian response to the horrors of war and the duties of citizenship that he required hospitalization for a period of deep depression in 1944. With the resolution of the war and his own personal crisis, Niebuhr addressed himself to the role of the church in the work of reconstruction. Having interpreted war as crucifixion, Niebuhr's search for signs of resurrection in its ending is not surprising, since dying and rising was for him the "logic" of God's ways with men. In a variety of published articles Niebuhr summoned the postwar churches to unite not on issues of faith and order but around efforts to attack world injustices and enlarge world community. The times called not for strategic withdrawal but for active participation in healing the wounds of men and nations.

These occasional pieces led to a sustained period of rethinking the role of the church and the nature of faith in relation to the world. In characteristic fashion Niebuhr condensed and crystallized his thinking in a comprehensive survey of the history of Christian ethics in what became his best-known book, *Christ and Culture* (1951).[13] In this book, he developed a marvelously concise and accurate typology of five different patterns of the church's relation to culture, ranging from total opposition to total accommodation. Niebuhr acknowledged a limited and strategic validity to each pattern, but his conclusions to this historical study clearly favor that mediating way which brings "Christ" and "Culture" together in a continuing process of transformation.

Niebuhr continued to explore the same set of problems from a different angle by focusing on the experience of human faith rather than on the varieties of Christian ethics. Here he placed the Christian life in the much broader context of seeing some form of faith as the basis of all social and cultural existence— political, economic, scientific, artistic and religious. The particular form of faith given through Jesus Christ, which Niebuhr called "radical faith," affirms the underlying worth and unity of all finite things because they have their ultimate being and value in one, infinite God.

Niebuhr expanded and refined these materials on faith through the fifties, dealing with them in lectures at several institutions and finally bringing them together in a large manuscript entitled "Faith on Earth: Essays on Human Confidence and Loyalty." [14] But the proposed publisher failed to appreciate the importance and originality of the larger part of the manuscript which dealt with the Christian's experience of coming to radical faith. All that was finally published, under the title *Radical Monotheism and Western Culture* (1960),[15] was Niebuhr's terse analysis of the three general forms of faith (polytheism, henotheism and radical monotheism) that are reflected in our culture's political, scientific, educational and religious activities and institutions. But here again Niebuhr is clear that radical faith means the continuing reformation of the individual and the society, of the church and the world.

Training persons for this ministry of reconciliation was always a primary concern for Niebuhr, since he was above all else a *teacher* of churchmen. From 1954 to 1956, he led a team study of theological education in the United States and Canada for the American Association of Theological Schools. Joined by Daniel Day Williams and James Gustafson, he conducted extensive surveys of the historical conceptions and educational training of the ministry as background for their recommendation of new guidelines for theological and pastoral education. These studies were published in two separate volumes, *The Ministry in Historical Perspectives* (1956) edited by Niebuhr and Williams, and *The Advancement of Theological Education* (1957) which was jointly authored by all three.[16] Finally, Niebuhr was given the task of developing and formulating the "sense of the meeting" for the study staff. From that duty came *The Purpose of the Church and Its Ministry* (1956) [17] which presented a reevaluation of the role of the church in American life, a fresh concept of the ministry and a restatement of the idea of a theological school. On each point Niebuhr stressed the church's "companionship" with the world, a companionship marked by mutual cooperation, instruction, repentance and conversion.

In the early sixties, Niebuhr turned his thoughts more directly to his lifelong preoccupation with Christian ethics. He further explored philosophical problems of the moral self in materials prepared for and given as the Robertson Lectures at the University of Glasgow and repeated at Cambridge University and the University of Bonn during a trip abroad in 1960. Related problems dealing with the "Christic form" of the moral self were presented in the Earl Lectures at the Pacific School of Religion in 1962. As retirement in 1963 drew near, Niebuhr began to bring together notes from his major lecture course in ethics at Yale. He probably planned to begin work that summer on what would have been his *magnum opus*, a comprehensive and systematic exposition of his ethics. But suddenly and unexpectedly H. Richard Niebuhr died on July 5, 1962. The world was thereby denied the full results of his forty-year career as teacher and writer in theological ethics.

But all that labor was not lost. There were after all three generations of students who had learned to do ethics under

him, many of whom have gone on to achieve distinction in that
field of study. Moreover, through the years students stenographi-
cally recorded Niebuhr's lectures in ethics, including one complete and verbatim account transcribed by a three-man team in
1952. Various sets of these notes have long circulated in mimeographed form among the Niebuhr literati, and an authorized set
will doubtless soon be published, along with other important
unpublished materials from the Niebuhr corpus.

Finally, what might be considered a kind of prolegomenon
to Niebuhr's ethics was published posthumously as *The Responsible Self* in 1962.[18] This volume, collected by his son
Richard R. and introduced by his colleague James Gustafson,
contains the lectures Niebuhr delivered in Europe in 1960 and
selections from the Earl Lectures of 1962. From this book, the
style and substance of Niebuhr's approach to ethics are evident.
Moral action and reflection are dynamic processes of transformation—"fitting responses" to what God is doing in all the
self's experiences and relationships.

The foregoing sketch of certain crucial influences, critical
junctures and changing emphases in Niebuhr's life lend biographical weight to the dynamic character of his reformation of
the message and life of faith. He worked out his thought about
God and man, life and death, sorrow and joy, in continuing response to public events and personal experiences. This is not to
say, however, that Niebuhr was an *ad hoc* thinker—responding
to each situation in spontaneous activism or intuitive understanding. Though his thinking remained "in solution" throughout his life, it was no process of unending flux. Certain bench
marks were achieved, certain problems were resolved. These
were, to be sure, largely formal in nature and confessional in
statement. Broadly speaking, they were solutions to two *procedural* questions: How can we think theologically in any situation? How can we act responsibly in any situation? But these
procedural questions must be settled at least provisionally before one can speak theologically or decide morally in this or
that concrete situation. For that reason, Niebuhr's theological
and ethical reflections do represent an important and lasting

contribution to the ongoing reformation of the church and world. Before analyzing these contributions in critical detail, however, the historical development of Niebuhr's theological method and ethical stance will be traced in the remaining chapters of Part One.

II. Reworking Theology

From the outset, Niebuhr's approach to the Christian faith was more practical than theoretical, more a matter of relationships than of beliefs. This bent is not surprising, given the theological parentage of his early training and ministry. On the German side was that strain of Protestant Liberalism exemplified by Harnack who interpreted Christianity primarily as a moral affair—as the brotherhood of man under the fatherhood of God. On the American side, the social gospel of Walter Rauschenbusch emphasized the social locus of sin and salvation in calling the church to build up the kingdom of God on earth. These emphases on bringing all personal relationships and social institutions under divine headship were to remain inseparably bonded and absolutely central in Niebuhr's understanding of the Christian faith throughout his career. But he soon became deeply dissatisfied with the reigning theology and ethics of both the German liberals and the American social gospel.

He began to doubt the *practical* power of these traditions to call forth anything more than a brotherhood of European manners, to establish anything more than a kingdom of American prosperity. He quickly surmised that these practical shortcomings were at base failures in understanding God. Their programs of human brotherhood were bourgeois because their view of God's fatherhood was sentimental. Their strategies of social transformation were parochial because their vision of God's sovereignty was uncritical. In other words, Niebuhr saw that their ethics were deficient because their theologies were inadequate. Therefore, he first addressed himself to the question of how we *know* God in order subsequently to deal with the problem of how we *serve* God.

A CHASTENED LIBERALISM

Niebuhr's reworking of his theological heritage began with his studies at Yale in the early 1920s. Of decisive importance was his doctoral dissertation on Ernst Troeltsch, the great turn-of-the-century German philosopher of religion and culture.[1] Through this study, Niebuhr faced problems and formed convictions which became a permanent part of his approach to Christian life and thought. At their center was a recognition and acceptance of the historicity and variety of all religious experiences and expressions, including those of the Christian faith.

As a philosopher of religion, Troeltsch had first dealt with the historical and cultural diversity of religion in a Kantian way, by detecting a rational core of universal sameness in all religions. But under the impact of the new sociological and psychological studies of religion of the times, Troeltsch radically revised his views to take account of the interplay of rational and nonrational, transcendental and cultural factors in all experiences and expressions of religion.[2] He still believed that the rational and the transcendental were really there in history but in a much more concealed and ambiguous way than religious rationalists (appealing to absolute reason) or supernaturalists (invoking special revelation) could admit. Put differently, although Troeltsch firmly believed in an Absolute God beyond the relativities of history, that Absolute God is known only through the relativities of history in a historically relative way. Not surprisingly, this realistic shift radically altered the style and content of Troeltsch's interpretation of Christianity. Troeltsch came to see Christianity as the normative synthesis of the values of Western culture, but by no means universally or eternally true. This cultural synthesis, being historically conditioned and limited, always remained open to critical revision and further development.

Niebuhr's appropriation of Troeltsch was by no means uncritical or imitative. Though the Troeltschian problematics of the relation between the Absolute and the relative, between monism and pluralism, became lifelong concerns for Niebuhr, in later years he would employ this tension in very different ways with very different results than did Troeltsch. Niebuhr's attack was to be consistently less philosophical and rationalistic, more theological and religious. This is not to say that all Niebuhr found in Troeltsch was a clear statement of the *problems* facing modern Christianity. The style of Troeltsch's scholarship and the depth of his faith made a lasting impression. Niebuhr found in Troeltsch an incomparable example of a willingness and ability to revise, a catholicity and appreciation of variety, a facility and inventiveness with typological constructs, a sensitivity and passion for community, a courage and acceptance of mortality, and a reverence and faith in the God who is beyond all finding out. More particularly, he found two decisive resources for beginning the reformulation of his own theological heritage. Troeltsch's relativism furnished a point of leverage against all uncritical identifications of the cause of God with the causes of men. Troeltsch's realism, which located religion in experiences and expressions of human value, suggested the way to distinguish between God's cause and the causes of men without completely severing them.

Niebuhr reinforced and refined these positive carryovers from Troeltsch through his study of a new American theological realism exemplified in his major professor at Yale, D. C. Macintosh.[3] Macintosh was highly critical of the eclecticism of nineteenth-century liberalism. God and man were too closely identified in that entire tradition. Primarily because of liberalism's concentration on religious *experience* as the object of

theological reflection, God too readily became little more than
the symbolic expression or ultimate sanction of a particular way
of life and social order. In remedy, Macintosh insisted that *God*
must be moved back to the center of religious concern and
theological reflection. This move, however, in no sense meant a
retreat from the moral and historical earnestness of liberal
theology. Christian thought and life must be centered in God,
but in God known and served "empirically"—in and through
personal and social, historical and cultural experience.

How then is faith and thought centered in God yet rooted in
experience? Drawing on the model of scientific explanation and
control, Macintosh argued that God's personal presence and
power may be discovered empirically with the aid of universal
values. God is at work, and faith is sure whenever and wherever experience manifests a "rationality, and beauty and goodness of personal life, individual and social, which we may
reasonably regard as valid ends, always, everywhere, and for
all persons." [4] Employing these universal values, Macintosh inductively developed "laws" of divine and human interaction
which provided the believer with "religious techniques" for
joining divine power and human interest.

While Niebuhr never emulated Macintosh's scientific theory
and "technology" of religious experience, he did welcome his
efforts to move God to the center of religious thought and life
and to interpret man's experience of God in terms of personal
and social values. He soon became convinced, however, that
neither Macintosh nor Troeltsch had succeeded in overcoming
the failures of German and American liberal theology. In the
final analysis, both men still defined faith in terms of values
known prior to or independent of the experience of Christian
faith, and each in his own way brought these norms of judgment
to the theological task. God was thereby still defined in terms
of ethical values which are somehow known apart from God
and, as such, still liable to become the cosmic supporter and
guarantor of some independently definable good. In short,
neither Troeltsch's nor Macintosh's approach fully and finally
"let God be God" in Christian understanding and practice.

Niebuhr's conviction that Troeltsch and Macintosh were not sufficiently critical of the liberal tradition was decisively influenced by a far more radical theological realism just emerging in Germany. Of central importance for his development were the so-called "crisis theologians," Karl Barth and Paul Tillich. Barth's revolt against liberal theology's whole line of march from Friedrich Schleiermacher to Ernst Troeltsch turned on that theology's "anthropocentric starting point." [5] By beginning with religious experience as the proper subject of theological reflection, these theologies compromised the sovereignty of God and minimized the sinfulness of man. Barth called for a radical reversal of all anthropocentric or experiential starting points in Christian theology. Nothing less than a total break between divine grace and human effort, between historical revelation and rational speculation, between supernatural faith and natural virtue—indeed, between *God* and *man*—could restore God as the sole object of faith and the proper subject of theology. The priority, power and purpose of humankind's salvation lies wholly with the "Wholly Other God."

In Barth's protesting theology, Niebuhr saw a "transcendental realism" bent on separating the reality of God from all rational ideas about him and all natural experiences of him. He valued the prophetic and iconoclastic power of Barth's shift of religion's center from man to God, and readily identified with his stress on the religious importance of God's judgment, of God's seeming opposition to all finite meaning and being. He also agreed with Barth on the necessity of the historical revelation of human faith and human good. But Niebuhr was quick to recognize that Barth's ontology (theory of being), epistemology (theory of knowledge), and soteriology (theory of salvation) were inimical to a *historical* realism.[6] By severing revelation from all human understanding and values, Barth's theology could only mean a rebirth of orthodoxy—a return to viewing faith dogmatically rather than practically, to believing revealed truths rather than personally experiencing God. For these reasons Niebuhr early tagged Barth's neoorthodoxy as a necessary but exaggerated protest against the anthropocentric methods and idolatrous tendencies of liberal theology.

In the writings of Paul Tillich, Niebuhr found a different version of German religious realism that was much more concerned with positive relationships between God and man *in* history.[7] Like Barth, Tillich laid heavy stress on the transcendence of God but, unlike Barth, he sought to locate that "otherness" within personal and cultural experience. Tillich's concern to relate the facts of history to the fact of God was closely allied to Ernst Troeltsch, in whom Tillich saw both greatness and failure as a theologian. Troeltsch's greatness as a theologian lay in his destruction of false absolutes in theology and philosophy and in his attempt to join the "Unconditional beyond history" and the "conditional within history" through his concept of the cultural synthesis. His failure as a theologian lay in the inadequate execution of these intentions. Tillich believed that Troeltsch compromised his views on relativism by too closely identifying the Absolute with the cultural synthesis of modern Europeanism. But even in failure, Tillich thought Troeltsch was of crucial importance for the future of theology. His efforts to relate the Unconditional to the conditional through cultural gestalts of meaning needed only to be revised not replaced.

Tillich sought that revision in terms of a distinction between two kinds of history—*chronos* which is sequential time and *kairos* which is fulfilled time. He argued that every moment of history (*chronos*) is related to God, although not every moment is aware of this relation. There are, however, those revelatory moments in history (*kairos*) when the Unconditional's relation to all history becomes explicit in ecstatic experiences of judgment and healing. *Kairos* marks those historical situations which become transparent to their own ultimate depth. Such historical revelations thereby become the remembered and anticipated means through which all historical events may be interpreted as situational expressions of Unconditional meaning and being. In this way, Tillich developed a theology of culture which draws on the normative content of particular events in history to discern the Unconditional depth and demand in every event of history.

The early Tillich's influence on Niebuhr's search for a new theological method was immense. This impact was due in part to the *historical* concreteness of Tillich's version of crisis theology. He underscored the positive rather than the negative side of God's otherness, the nearness rather than the remoteness of God's transcendence. Perhaps even more important for Niebuhr, Tillich's constructive approach to the facts of history and the fact of God had been developed in direct response to Troeltsch. By interpreting Christianity in a philosophical framework less static and abstract than Troeltsch's philosophical idealism, Tillich overcame a number of shortcomings in Troeltsch's formulation of Christian faith. He was freed from Troeltsch's reluctance to claim or to look for normative revelations of God in the particular events of history. He was able to search for structures and purposes in history more encompassing than Troeltsch's cultural syntheses, without losing sight of the situational character of every manifestation of Unconditional depth and demand within history. Most important of all, he substituted for Troeltsch's appeal to rational judgment, as the means by which the Unconditional is discerned in conditional events and experiences, an intuitive, experiential faith. Thus Niebuhr found in Tillich a discerning critique and a constructive alternative to Troeltsch. Unlike Barth's "transcendental realism," Tillich's "historical realism" offered Niebuhr a ready-made theological synthesis which stressed the independence and priority of God, while still seeing present events and patterns of history as expressions and experiences of that very God.

Yet Niebuhr became no disciple of Tillich's catalytic theology. He did carry over its correlational structure and cultural seriousness as permanent features of his way of doing theology and ethics. But Niebuhr early surmised that Tillich's mystical, intuitive conception of faith and his theology's formal, abstract language of ontology made God more ineffable and faith more interior than American religious sensibilities allowed. A theology appropriate and relevant to the American scene required a conceptuality more self-consciously biblical and relational than Tillich afforded. Indeed, Niebuhr was convinced that German realism needed American theology's moral earnestness as much as American realism needed German theology's metaphysical otherness.[8] Human practicalities were as neglected in German theology as divine priorities were compromised in American. Thus, Niebuhr was left with the problem of how to combine the empirical and anthropocentric interests of the American realists with the transcendental and theocentric commitments of the German realists.

Niebuhr was under no illusions about how difficult that task would prove to be. He was convinced, along with the German realists, of the necessity to assert the independence of God, the relativity of historical experience, and the pervasive presence of evil. But he was equally convinced that the independence of God from experience need not entail his remoteness from experience, that the relativity of historical experience need not imply the absence of some absolute point of reference, and that the presence of evil in subtle and pervasive forms need not prove the absence of good.[9] In other words, Niebuhr was unwilling to abandon the experiential concreteness and social passion that characterized liberal theology in its various German and American expressions, even in the face of the devastating critiques of that tradition by the crisis theologians. He stubbornly believed that the theological and ethical, critical and constructive interests of these juxtaposed traditions could be and must be combined.

Such combination, however, meant more than simple annexation. German theology and American ethics, German theocentrism and American anthropocentrism could not be joined like collected essays in a book and thereby become a whole. What was needed was a "third piece"—a mediating element that would change both traditions by revealing and completing the meaning of the partial picture that appears in each. Precisely what that "third piece" would be was not yet clear to Niebuhr, but in the 1930s he wrote a series of crucial methodological essays that staked out three critical desiderata.[10] Such a new theological synthesis must be *empirical* while maintaining the independence of God from believing experience, *valuational* while preserving the priority of God for determining the content of believing experience, and *historical* while accounting for the

presence of God to believing experience. It must be all this and
more. It must capture the enthusiasms and speak with the
cadences of American Christianity.

A NEW SYNTHESIS

Curiously enough, the major impetus for achieving this new
theological synthesis came largely from Niebuhr's historical
studies in the mid-1930s. In the 1920s and early thirties, Niebuhr's personal experiences and theological explorations had
converged in one fundamental certainty—the sovereignty of
God. Closely associated with this certainty were two other convictions—the universality of human sinfulness and the mystery
of divine graciousness.[11] Like others of his theological generation, Niebuhr recognized that these cardinal notes were also at
the center of both the social past and the theological tradition
that liberal theology had rejected. Thus Niebuhr went back behind his own liberal heritage to study what he later called "the
Great Tradition" in theology, especially Augustine, Thomas
Aquinas, Calvin, Luther, Pascal and Jonathan Edwards.[12] His
study of these "theologians of the sovereignty of God" height-
ened his sense of the divine prevenience in all events and
processes, and strengthened his conviction of the full compati-
bility of divine sovereignty and human responsibility. But these
same studies also intensified the problematic at the core of his
personal religion and his theological reflection—the question of
the *goodness* of the God who rules a world as tragic as ours. As
a consequence, the christological problem became ever more
important and urgent in Niebuhr's thinking. What finally is the
meaning of the disclosure that God rules through the Cross?

Even more important for Niebuhr's development was a two-
year study of American Christianity in connection with his
classes and seminars at Yale. Niebuhr undertook this study because he believed that theology must always speak in and to a
concrete situation, and that no such situation can be rightly
understood apart from its historical development. These lectures
were shortly thereafter published as one of Niebuhr's most re-

markable books—*The Kingdom of God in America* (1937). In this book Niebuhr interpreted America as "an experiment in constructive Protestantism." He defined "constructive Protestantism" as the effort to find practical patterns of personal, social and institutional life which embody the sovereignty of God. He believed that this concern to incarnate the kingdom of God in total life lay at the heart of the Reformation, but that only in the New World, where established religions and regimes were completely absent, did circumstances permit its full and free development. But his studies convinced him that this development was by no means uniform and unambiguous.

Niebuhr saw in Protestantism's unifying principle of the kingdom of God three distinguishable themes:

> The Christian faith in the kingdom of God is a threefold thing. Its first element is confidence in the divine sovereignty which, however hidden, is still the reality behind and in all realities. A second element is the conviction that in Jesus Christ the hidden kingdom was not only revealed in a convincing fashion but also began a special and new career among men, who had rebelled against the true law of their nature. The third element is the direction of life to the coming kingdom in power or to the redemption of the self-sufficient world.[13]

Niebuhr further argued that while these themes are complementary and compatible, one or another seems to dominate the others in any given historical time and place. Thus, in America the early Puritan settlers were dominated by the first theme— "the living reality of God's present rule, not only in human spirits, but also in the world of nature and human history." The theme of the kingdom of Christ emerged to prominence in the Great Awakenings of the eighteenth century with their vivid recovery of the transforming power of Jesus Christ to convert "minds and hearts to the love of God and of man in God." In the nineteenth century, the third theme of the "Coming Kingdom" became paramount in an explosion of religious and social millenarianisms bent on preparing and pressing for the full realization of the kingdom of God in the present. By the first decades of the twentieth century, Niebuhr found that these various expressions of the kingdom of God had been thoroughly institutionalized in evangelical revivalism and fundamentalism, and secularized in liberal religiosity and humanitarianism. The former displayed a self-confidence and self-righteousness which could not help but evoke a reaction from those who discerned how relative and confining were their visions of the kingdom of God. As for the latter, to repeat one of Niebuhr's most oft-quoted comments, "a God without wrath brought men without sin into a kingdom without judgment through the ministrations of a Christ without a cross." [14] The living current of the kingdom of God had been frozen into a rigidity lacking human warmth and divine life.

Niebuhr insisted, however, that these petrifications and perversions of the early twentieth century were by no means absent from earlier centuries of the American experiment. Puritanism hardened into the Half-way Covenant, and Quakerism into birthright membership. The Great Awakenings shattered these fetters and restored the kingdom's dynamic only to settle into theological defensiveness, petty moralism, denominational exclusivism and blatant nationalism. The denomination and the nation became the chosen, favored people of God. Against this easy identification of Christ's kingdom with church and state, the nineteenth century's call to bring in the Coming Kingdom evoked new life. But this new life in turn lapsed into an orthodox, otherworldly individualism and a liberal, evolutionary optimism. Even the social gospel which appeared toward the end of the nineteenth century as a genuine heir of the dynamic Coming Kingdom did not fully escape this preoccupation with the conservation and extension of American political and ecclesiastical institutions. In short, Niebuhr saw an inevitable rhythm of fluidity and fixity, of reformation and institutionalization of the kingdom of God in American history.

Niebuhr appreciated the ambiguity of these inevitable crystallizations of new religious movements into codes, organizations and creeds. He recognized that at best they were genuine efforts to conserve for postrevolutionary generations the gains made by the new movement. They consolidated the gains of the revolutionary epoch and put them into forms that could be transmitted to children and children's children. "Without such stabilization and conservation the great movements would have passed like storms at sea, leaving behind them nothing but the wreckage of the earlier establishments they had destroyed." [15] Yet, Niebuhr insisted, the establishment of ecclesiastical and political forms of a revolutionary movement of faith can never conserve without betraying the movement from which they proceed. The forms begotten are static, whereas the parent movement had been dynamic.

Thus, Niebuhr's historical study of the kingdom of God in America decisively confirmed his abiding conviction that the reformation of church and society *is* the continuing imperative of the Christian faith. That imperative is not a call to *cease* fashioning institutional forms of the kingdom, but to *continue* developing new sacred and secular expressions of it in the now of every new generation.

Niebuhr gained far more from this study than a historical confirmation of his conviction that Christian faith means permanent *metanoia*. He also discovered that his own social gospel heritage and concerns were by no means incommensurate with the lifeblood of American Christianity. Man's responsibility for building a "world without walls" is profoundly rooted in the tradition of the sovereignty of God. A final contribution of this study was a deepened appreciation of Jesus Christ as the historical mediator of that radical faith in God which transforms the self and the world. But these lessons were nothing less than the three themes of the kingdom of God in America—sovereignty, grace, hope! What Niebuhr learned in his study of American Christianity was the necessity of bringing all three themes together in a dynamic and dialectical balance; the loss of one or another of these elements compromises the full understanding and practice of Christian faith.

Niebuhr sought precisely that balance in his crowning theological statement, *The Meaning of Revelation* (1941). In the

preface, he pointed out that his study rests on three fundamental
convictions:

> The first is the conviction that self-defense is the most prevalent
> source of error in all thinking and perhaps especially in theology
> and ethics. I cannot hope to have avoided this error in my ef-
> forts to state Christian ideas in confessional terms only, but I
> have at least tried to guard against it. The second idea is that the
> great source of evil in life is the absolutizing of the relative,
> which in Christianity takes the form of substituting religion, reve-
> lation, church or Christian morality for God. The third convic-
> tion, which becomes most explicit in the latter part of this essay
> but underlies the former part, is that Christianity is "permanent
> revolution" or *metanoia* which does not come to an end in this
> world, this life or this time. Positively stated these three convic-
> tions are that man is justified by grace, that God is sovereign,
> and that there is an eternal life.[16]

These three convictions are of course restatements of the three
elements Niebuhr had uncovered in his study of American
Christianity. Their reformulation and combination gave him
what he needed to bring his search for a mediating theological
method to fruition. He had come to see that the mediating element required to conjoin the anthropocentrism of liberal theology and the theocentrism of crisis theology was christological
in substance. Those complementary articulations of Christian
faith could only come together in a theology of revelation. But
that revelation must be at once the mediation of God and the
transformation of man in *actual* history. God must be known
and served in and through the concrete histories of selves and
communities without being collapsed into or separated from
those histories. In *The Meaning of Revelation,* Niebuhr sketched
out a way to meet those demands by bringing together sovereign
God and sinful man in an unending and inescapable process of
historical transformation. Here at last the reformer has a theological method to match the religious mandate that he had so
keenly felt and ardently advocated for a dozen years—*reformation as continuing imperative!*

This revolutionary thrust at the heart of Niebuhr's way of

doing theology came to clear expression in *The Meaning of Revelation* in the way he handled the three stubborn problems that confront any contemporary theology of revelation—the relationship between the relative and the absolute in history, between scientific and religious historical understanding, and between natural religion and historical faith.[17] While a full analysis of Niebuhr's solution to these problems must await the next section, a brief description here will serve to conclude and confirm this sketch of the reformer's search for a reforming theological method.

Niebuhr dealt with the first problem by correlating human historicity and divine sovereignty. Human beings are historical beings whose ways of thinking, feeling and acting are always conditioned by a particular society with its own distinctive past. Even man's faith-relationship to God is immersed in this radical historicity. Every encounter with God happens in the context of some historical community of persons whose perceptions and responses of faith are formed by the founding events and on-going life of that communal history. But, against all claims that any single communal history mediates the full and final truth of God, Niebuhr contended that God is not and cannot be so contained. Human finitude and sin being what they are, no historical community perfectly embodies its experiences of God in life or deed, in scripture or symbol. Even if perfect embodiment were possible, such experiences would necessarily still bear the limitations of their situational givenness, since historical relevance implies historical relativism.

Thus, for Niebuhr the Absolute God is always and only experienced in a historically and religiously relative way. Nonetheless, it is *God* that is experienced thereby and not simply the believer's inner consciousness, social milieu or sacred symbols. Seen in this light, Christians are those for whom Jesus Christ is that event in history which founds and funds their community's distinctive experiences of God. "Theology, then, must begin *in* Christian history and *with* Christian history because it has no other choice; in this sense it is forced to begin with revelation, meaning by that word simply historic faith." [18]

The historical and religious necessity for Christians to start

with Jesus Christ raises the second problem mentioned above—
the matter of the relation between a scientific and a religious
understanding of historical events. How can God be revealed
through historical events which are themselves subject to scientific investigation and explanation? Niebuhr spelled out his
solution to this problem in terms of a distinction between external history and internal history. "External history" means
the past as it is known by the spectator who investigates it from
the outside to determine its causal relationships, emergent structures, recurrent patterns and distinctive features. This kind of
dispassionate investigation by scientific historians can never discover, much less demonstrate, what Christians claim about Jesus
Christ as a special manifestation of God and man. Such claims
rest on an entirely different kind of historical understanding
and relationship to the past.

In contrast to the outside observer's view, history can also be
known from the inside by participants who remember certain
events because of their continuing impact on their lives. Such
participants may include more than contemporaries or eyewitnesses to such events, if their meanings are embodied in story
and deed by an ongoing, remembering community. Thus, the
significance of Jesus Christ is not that once upon a time there
was a special Son of God whose life and teachings can be known
through historical research (the Historical Jesus). Nor is Jesus
Christ a spiritual being who communicates directly with human
hearts and minds today (the Resurrected Christ). Rather, Jesus
Christ is that historic one in the living memory of the Christian
community who was and is the mediator of a new relationship
between God and men. For Niebuhr, only this kind of historical
remembrance—where the lives of contemporary participants in
a historic community are decisively shaped by and through its
remembered past—is revelatory. Christians are those who tell
and live the story of what happened and happens to that community of believers which remembers Jesus Christ as revealer
and reconciler of God and man.

For Niebuhr, revelation is mediated through the remembered
Christ in the remembering community. The content of that

revelation, however, is *God*—not the inner awareness or exemplary life of the historical Jesus (his messianic consciousness) nor the common life or interpretive vision of the early
church (the apostolic witness). Furthermore, God's personal
presence and power are not experienced in some purely inward
or mystical way by contemporary believers. Rather, God is encountered in and through the concrete interpretations and practical activities of their daily lives. But this double mediation of
revelation through the believing community's remembered past
and the contemporary believer's experienced present brings up
the third problem mentioned previously—the question of the
relation between natural religion and historic faith. How is the
content of revelation related to all those perceptions of human
nature and destiny which are held prior to or outside of revelation's historically mediated encounter with God?

Niebuhr dealt with this problem in terms of the transformation of natural religion and the universalization of historic
faith. Religion is given with life itself in the sense that all
human beings live out of *some* sense of life's ultimate meaning
and purpose. Just as men require an "animal faith" in the
dependability of their sensory experience to exist as bodies in
the world, so they require a "religious faith" in the worthwhile-
ness of their practical endeavors to exist as selves in history. For
Niebuhr, this natural religion is neither merely confirmed nor
contradicted by revelation. "Revelation is not the development
and not the elimination of our natural religion; it is the *revolution* of the religious life." [19] Revelation is that occasion in communal and personal history which transforms our natural sense
of deity and duty, of meaning and purpose.

The effect of revelation, then, is not to establish a *sui generis*
body of beliefs or community of believers but to transform the
ideas and relationships men already have. Revelation furnishes
new patterns and paradigms by means of which historic faith
can and must rationally reinterpret and morally reorder the
world. This very reconstruction, however, requires historic faith
to acknowledge that God's transformative work is not limited
to or even defined by its own historic encounter with God. The

God revealed to historic faith is the One Person who wills and works a permanent revolution in every time and place. Historic faith is thus compelled to admit that it has the clues but not the keys to the kingdom. In faithfulness to those clues, it bears witness in word and deed to a universal process of conversion going on among all peoples and within all perspectives, such that finally God might be all in all, and all God's creatures one.

To bring these three skeins together in a summary way, Niebuhr believed that Christian theology can speak only from a limited point of view in history and faith. It can only tell what it sees from that limited standpoint by retelling the story of its remembered past and envisioned future. But that story is not limited to the Christian community's historic revelation and common life. What Christians see in and through Jesus Christ is the sovereign God gathering together all creatures great and small in one world without end. Christian theology's task, then, is to help the Christian cadre understand and undertake its historic role in that permanent revolution which is God's universal kingdom.

That such a theology would be practical through and through is obvious—practical in the double sense that man's primary experience of God is relational rather than doctrinal, and that his primary duty before God is ethical rather than liturgical. Indeed, as pointed out earlier, Niebuhr's search for a new theological synthesis was prompted by moral concern. He had found liberal and crisis theologies lacking precisely at the point of their inability to furnish a theological ethics at once distinctively Christian and culturally relevant. Niebuhr's long search for a viable theological method was aimed at a theological synthesis that could so ground and guide the Christian moral life. But stating the matter this way could be misleading, since it might seem to suggest that Niebuhr's development of his moral stance came only after his theological quest was complete. Nothing could be further from the truth. Niebuhr's theological position was worked out in close relation to his teaching and research, pronouncements and publications on Christian ethics during these years. Though never identical, theology and ethics were *always* inseparable for him. Thus his search for a theological method was organically related to his search for an ethical stance. In fact, his search for a viable Christian ethics started earlier and lasted longer than his quest for a new theological synthesis. That historical process will be traced in the next chapter to recount Niebuhr's development in full.

III. Rethinking Ethics

Prior to entering Yale in 1922, Niebuhr published three articles in his denomination's *Magazin für evangelische Theologie und Kirche*. Two of these dealt with the church's moral obligations toward society.[1] These were rather typical Social Gospel nostrums. They summoned the church to embody as well as preach the higher righteousness of the Sermon on the Mount (the infinite worth of the individual and the duty of sacrificial love) by way of joining and ameliorating the labor movement's struggle for economic and social justice.

This simplistic and organic view of Christian virtue and social righteousness was soon undermined by Niebuhr's studies at Yale. Of decisive importance in this regard was his doctoral dissertation on Ernst Troeltsch. From Troeltsch, Niebuhr gained a new grasp of the relativity and complexity of the church's moral relations to society. Troeltsch's critical-empirical work showed him how morally diverse and often perverse were the kinds of values which compete for men's loyalties in every culture—political, economic, artistic, scientific and religious. Troeltsch's constructive-philosophical formulations impressed him with how important a reconciliation or synthesis of these cultural values is to personal well-being and social stability. Niebuhr clearly saw that the combination of these critical and constructive concerns required a radically new moral stance and strategy for the church. But Troeltsch's way of combining them was never entirely convincing or compatible to Niebuhr. The root of Niebuhr's dissatisfaction with Troeltsch lay in the latter's rationalism. For Troeltsch, relative values had their reality and unity only in the Absolute God beyond history who lures each historically relative culture toward its ideal coherence and completion. That invisible and inevitable process can only be discerned, however, *in* the values themselves *through* a philosophical explication of human thought's secret alliance with divine reality. Thus, although Troeltsch acknowledged the historical relativity of all cultural values while grounding their reality in God, he nevertheless did not find a way to the reality and will of God apart from cultural values. Troeltsch was the epitome of the tendency in liberal theology to discern God's presence in history (past and present) through some measure or criterion arising within contemporary experience itself.

Why this should have proven troublesome to Niebuhr at this time is not revealed in his study of Troeltsch. Criticisms of Troeltsch in the dissertation deal largely with tensions and difficulties internal to Troeltsch's thought, and Niebuhr offers no constructive alternative. But from publications that started appearing immediately after the completion of his doctoral studies, we can surmise that Niebuhr was already being deeply influenced by the new theological realism in Germany and America which stressed God's independence and priority over all personal and cultural values. The work of Barth and Tillich in Germany and of Macintosh and Wieman in America raised critical questions in Niebuhr's mind about liberal theology's use of any experiential a priori (whether psychological, moral or rational) to discern and describe God's presence and purpose in human history. As we saw in the previous chapter, these realistic strictures did not compel Niebuhr to abandon liberal theology's empirical and valuational approach to Christian faith. But they did press him to differentiate more clearly between God and experience, revelation and reason, church and society in both theology and ethics.

SEPARATING THE CHURCH

Niebuhr launched his search for a new method of ethical reflection by trying to bring together the moral priorities of the liberals and the transcendental preoccupations of the realists. More exactly, Troeltsch's historical and social analysis coupled with the new biblical and theocentric realism gave Niebuhr double leverage on the culture-bound character of the American religious ethos. The first sign of his new appreciation of the steepness of the ethics of Jesus and the difficulty of realizing the kingdom of God on earth appeared in a remarkable essay entitled "Back to Benedict" (1925).[2] In this article, published the year following graduation from Yale, Niebuhr proposed a withdrawal of the church from culture. As the monk Benedict challenged the extreme church-world compromise of his time by radically separating the two, so a new *monasticism* offered one way—perhaps the only way—for the contemporary church to overcome its captivity to the nationalistic and capitalistic values of American society. Niebuhr duly noted the lopsidedness of monastic other-worldliness, but he surmised that precisely such overemphasis was needed to counter the lopsided this-worldliness of American Christianity. Theological and practical dualisms have their place and value if they break up those monisms which reduce spirit to matter, church to state, discipleship to citizenship, virtue to success. But this monastic summons to the church represented no change in Niebuhr's mind about the Christian's responsibility for society or the church's role in the synthesizing of cultural values. Withdrawal from the world was seen only as a *strategy* of renewal, as the only way the church could once again engage the world with the promise and the demand of the kingdom of God. The church as it was— fractured by partisan differences, immersed in cultural compromises—possessed neither the will nor the way to fulfill its moral responsibilities to the individual or the society.

Niebuhr developed this call for a principled separation of the church from all compromising relations with culture more fully in his first book, *The Social Sources of Denominationalism* (1929). The burden of Niebuhr's ethical concern at this time was how to reform and unify the churches in order that they might play their unifying and reforming role in culture. His research convinced him that denominational differences were less theological than they were historical, social and ethical. Individuals and groups are not defined primarily by ideas or constituted primarily by choice. Rather, they are resultants of such complex determinants as economic standing, class status, educational achievement, ethnic heritage, racial identity, political affiliation, sectional history and nationalistic identity. Patiently and perceptively exploring this complexity, Niebuhr intermingled historical analysis and prophetic criticism of "the ethical failure of the divided church." At bottom he saw pluralism of values and self-defensiveness as the causes of this malady, and moral paralysis and cultural disintegration as its consequences.[3]

Niebuhr concluded his diagnosis with a one-chapter guarded prognosis of the church's ethical failure. He pointed the way out through a Troeltschian synthesis of cultural values under the unifying power of some compelling and integrating ideal. But whence this supreme center? Denominational Christianity offered little hope for a common ethics and worldview, since it seemed incapable of establishing such harmony in its own structure. European crisis theology was less culturally compromised, but its blanket condemnation of all cultural and religious striving and its other-worldly faith rendered it irrelevant to the social task of Christianity. Niebuhr underscored the importance of crisis theology's insistence that the kingdom of God transcends all the relative versions of that ideal for which men work. But he insisted that there must be some relation between those relative achievements and the absolute fact of the kingdom. To refer men to some transcendental sphere or to some eschatological miracle for the attainment of divine rule, while meantime condemning all efforts to work out human salvation as best men can, reduces "religion to an ethical anodyne." [4]

Not finding the ethical power to shape a new synthesis of

cultural values in either denominational Christianity or crisis
theology, Niebuhr *did* reaffirm his conviction that the Christianity of the Gospels contains what is required for such a synthesis.

Its purpose is not the foundation of an ecclesiastical institution
or the proclamation of a metaphysical creed, though it seeks the
formation of a divine society and presupposes the metaphysics of
a Christlike God. Its purpose is the revelation to men of their
potential childhood to the Father and their possible brotherhood
with each other. That revelation is made not in terms of dogma
but of life, above all in the life of Christ. His sonship and his
brotherhood, as delineated in the gospel, are not the example
which men are asked to follow if they will, but rather the demonstration of that character of ultimate reality which they can ig-
nore only at the cost of their souls.[5]

This ideal, Niebuhr stated, is the secret goal of every great
religion, of every serious philosophy and indeed of every yearn-
ing heart. But he remained convinced that it could be proclaimed only by a church which transcends the partisan divisions
of the world and portends a universal fellowship of reconciliation. He saw such a church in the churches, becoming manifest again and again in moments of genuine reformation only to
be submerged once more in divisions and compromises. Making that latent church manifest again was the only road toward
unity for Christendom and for the world. That road, Niebuhr
avowed, could only be traveled by turning away from all loyalties that deny the inclusiveness of divine love and by turning to
"the eternal values of the Kingdom of God that is among us." [6]
Niebuhr's prescriptions for an ailing church were largely
voiced in the language of Troeltschian cultural synthesis and
social gospel utopianism. But a shift in the *theological* basis of
moral responsibility already can be discerned in Niebuhr's
wistful-sounding conclusion to *The Social Sources of Denominationalism.* Finally, Christian morality and cultural unity center
in that ultimate reality decisively revealed in Christ, who
wills and works a universal commonwealth of being and value.

How exactly to maintain God's centrality, Christ's authority, and the church's fidelity in defining and creating that kingdom of life and love was far from clear either theologically or ethically for Niebuhr at this time. Yet this book closes on a new note beyond Troeltsch and the social gospel. It signaled Niebuhr's growing confidence in the reality of a personal God and the normativeness of an historical revelation as the basis for Christian moral responsibility.

Over the next half dozen years Niebuhr's theological efforts to explicate this new sense of a historically revealed and historically active God were paralleled by a moral stance that was dominantly iconoclastic and quietistic. He continued his call for the church to withdraw from all compromising alliances without and to overcome all partisan differences within. Niebuhr dared hope that both might come about through the revitalization of the worldwide ecumenical movement following World War I, since at this time he still believed that the gospel of the kingdom required a supernational church transcending all partisan differences and parochial loyalties. But ever more clearly Niebuhr saw that such purity and unity required a revolution of the church's loyalties and priorities. The root cause of the church's cultural captivity and communal disarray was *idolatry*—a centering of values in something or some things other than God. Thus, in a variety of publications—sermons, lectures, essay, books—Niebuhr scored the churches for their false faith and summoned them away from their false gods. This trenchant moral iconoclasm was most clearly voiced in Niebuhr's joint authorship of *The Church Against the World* (1935), where he vividly portrayed God's judgment on the gods of cultural faith reverenced by church and world alike—capitalism, nationalism and anthropocentrism. From these the churches must be freed to be the church.

Against such attachments, Niebuhr's counsels of withdrawal were not only radically separatist but also quietistic. In a celebrated exchange of articles with his brother Reinhold over the proper Christian response to the Japanese invasion of Manchuria, he advocated the "meaningful inactivity" of repentance and forgiveness while God works out his judging and redeeming way in this great tragedy.[7] But even in this most extreme statement, Niebuhr's quietism was not pacifistic. His calls for separation and inaction were not so much counsels of Christian perfection as they were acknowledgments of human imperfection. During the early thirties, Niebuhr's emerging understanding of the interface of divine sovereignty and human sinfulness came down heavily on the necessity of *divine* liberation and transformation of human life. The false gods must be destroyed before the true God can be apprehended. Sinful man has no choice but to "wait upon the Lord" to be saved.

Furthermore, for Niebuhr this understanding carried more than the weight of studied agreement with the theologians of the sovereignty of God that he was reading at this time. His coming to this conviction had the impact and force of a personal conversion.[8] God is the One beyond the many, the final source of all human peril *and* power, since all things are in his hands. Thus, for reasons strategic, theological and deeply personal, Niebuhr's initial calls for submission and service to this mighty God stressed "the grace of doing nothing" while God works out his judgment and renewal in history. Only with the fuller development of the theological implications of his new grasp of divine sovereignty and human sinfulness would Niebuhr clearly see how God has enlisted "these unlikely beings, these human animals, ourselves, in his cause, the cause of universal creation and universal redemption." [9]

Notwithstanding, even in the early thirties Niebuhr's call for withdrawal remained strategic rather than programmatic. His new sense of the sovereignty of God and sinfulness of man led him to stress the discontinuities between divine grace and human effort, but he never intended their separation. Even in his most iconoclastic and quietistic pronouncements, his critical remonstrances always intended constructive consequences. These constructive concerns for the renewal of both personal *and* social existence, for the reformation of both church *and* world moved to the center of Niebuhr's developing thought in the late thirties and early forties.

TRANSFORMING THE WORLD

The decisive move toward a more positive and ameliorative moral relationship between the church and the world commenced with Niebuhr's preparation and publication of *The Kingdom of God in America* (1937). In the preface, Niebuhr acknowledged the imbalance of the approach to religion and culture that had dominated his thinking since *The Social Sources of Denominationalism.* That book had illumined the church as an institution but not as a movement, had explained its denominational diversity but not its religious unity, had exposed its dependence on culture but not its transcendence of culture. But a closer study of the history of American Protestantism convinced Niebuhr that the Christianity-culture coin had two faces. In *The Kingdom of God in America,* Niebuhr explored the other face—that "constructive Protestantism" which molds culture instead of being merely molded by it.[10]

As we saw above, this study pivoted on the centrality of the vision of the kingdom of God in American Christianity. Niebuhr found that the kingdom of God meant different things in different periods—"sovereignty of God" in the early period, "reign of Christ" in the awakening period, and "kingdom on earth" in the most recent period. Niebuhr saw a creative moral vitality emerge in each period as the theological idea of the kingdom was given fresh expression. But he also found that no period escaped turning its distinctive vision of the kingdom of God into an instrument of self-protection and self-advancement. This perception of both the power and the perversion of these three ideas convinced him that they were not three divergent ideas but that they belonged together. "Kingdom on earth without sovereignty of God and reign of Christ was meaningless, as the last two were incomplete without it and without each other." [11] In short, Niebuhr came to see that Christian ethics as well as Christian theology must find a way of holding together God's sovereignty, Christ's authority and man's responsibility in a continuing process of personal and social transformation.

This study of American Christianity brought about two profound changes in Niebuhr's understanding of the relation between the church and the world. First was the conviction that
Christianity must be understood as a movement rather than as
an institution. The "true church" is an organic movement of
all those who are called out to seek and serve the One God.
To be sure, institutions have their necessary place in that seeking and serving, but that place is instrumental rather than con-
stitutive. Furthermore, the church as institution is only one
among other cultural institutions (political, economic, educational, artistic) which give concrete expression and embodiment
to the "true church."

Second, Niebuhr was convinced that Christianity as a movement cannot be represented strictly as an other-worldly or as a
this-worldly process, nor yet as a static dualism of the two
complementing or paralleling one another. The relation between sovereign God revealed in Christ and sinful world transformed through Christ requires a dialectical movement of
worship and work in the life of the Christian and of the church.
No individual person or historical institution can ever bring
this movement between the other-worldly and the this-worldly
to completion—"only God can provide synthesis." [12] But each
individual and group can do its worship and work with full
recognition of their partial and incomplete character and with
full faith in the wholeness of God and God's kingdom which
makes the partial work significant. In other words, Niebuhr
abandoned all expectations and exhortations for some ideally
pure and united church as God's instrument of renewal.[13] He
came to see that the church is only one part of human culture,
and like other parts is subject to a constant process of reformation and deformation, of *metanoia* and fall. The problem of the
church is less a matter of separating itself from the idolatries of
the world than dealing with its own idolatries. Thus the reformation of the church and the reformation of the world must proceed apace as a permanent revolution of the world of culture
(man's achievement) within the world of grace (God's Kingdom).

Niebuhr worked out these new convictions about Christian commitment and secular involvement over the next dozen years in his courses on the history and types of Christian ethics at Yale and in publications dealing with a variety of issues on moral responsibility. The shape of Niebuhr's approach to Christian ethics first clearly emerged in his contribution to a collection of essays edited by Kenneth Scott Latourette, *The Gospel, the Church and the World* (1946).[14] Niebuhr's essay, entitled "The Responsibility of the Church for Society," foreshadows his distinctive interpretation of Christian ethics in terms of responsibility and response. Niebuhr argued that moral responsibility is a universal feature of the social life of men. Every human community requires its members to be responsible for each other in the common life. But that stewardship is always determined by a prior response to some shared interest which constitutes and characterizes the community as such. In other words, what men are responsible *for* in a community is always determined by what they are responsive *to* as a community. All human communities compare and contrast in terms of this double movement of "response to" and "responsibility for."

Given this structure of moral responsibility, *Christian* responsibility is constituted and characterized by the Christian community's response to the God in whom its common life centers. This God, Niebuhr insisted, is no tribal deity presiding over a family of the favored few either in heaven or on earth. Rather, the God revealed in Christ is the One Lord of heaven and earth who includes "all realms of being" in a reign of merciful and redeeming love. Response to this universal and redemptive God enjoins responsibility for his inclusive and regenerative kingdom. Such responsibility, Niebuhr further contended, is incompatible with a spiritualism limited to immaterial goods, with a moralism that values only the virtuous man or nation, with an individualism that disregards mankind as a whole or its societies, and with all idolatries that substitute some finite concern for God as the center and source of life's value.[15]

Drawing on this analysis of Christian responsibility, Niebuhr was able to define the church-world problem more incisively than heretofore. He scored the approaches to religion and culture of "the worldly church" and of "the isolated church" for their respective failures to maintain the double movement of Christian responsibility. The worldly church, so typical of liberal Protestantism and the American social gospel, wrongly defines the "to whom" of responsibility by making the church responsible to the society for which it is accountable. But substituting any human society for God, whether conceived of nationalistically or humanistically, is ruinous to morality as well as faith before a sovereign God. By contrast the isolated church, whether sanctioned by orthodox or neoorthodox theologies, wrongly defines the "for what" of responsibility by making the church responsible to God only for itself. But limiting accountability to the Christian church, whether conceived of denominationally or ecumenically, equally distorts faith and morality before the Lord of heaven and earth. Against these two forms of "irresponsible religion," Niebuhr maintained that the responsible church and the responsible self must live in the midst of a double movement from the world to God and from God to the world. "The relation to God and the relation to society must neither be confused with each other as is the case in social religion, nor separated from each other as is the case in Christian isolationism; they must be maintained in the unity of responsibility *to* God *for* the neighbor." [16]

Niebuhr tested and further refined his understanding of the relation between Christian commitment and secular involvement in his best-known book, *Christ and Culture* (1951). This book, which condensed years of study and teaching devoted to the history and typology of Christian ethics, examined Christianity's typical responses to the church-world problem. Characterizing this problem as the relation between "Christ" and "Culture," Niebuhr delineated five definable positions. The first type, "Christ against Culture," *excludes* culture as an area of positive activity on the part of God and of believers, since all culture is seen to be under the reign of evil. Niebuhr named the second approach "Christ of Culture" since it *accommodates* Christian truth and value to the best knowledge and highest norms of culture.[17]

Niebuhr found numerous examples of these two positions throughout Christian history beginning with primitive Christianity. He affirmed their historical importance as strategic correctives and one-sided directives in the continuing dialectic between Christ and culture through the centuries. But Niebuhr judged both positions finally to be theologically and ethically deficient. As such, neither the separation nor the assimilation of Christ and culture has ever dominated Christian thought and life as a whole. Rather, the Christian majority has always sought to hold Christ and culture together in some way that mediates between those two extremes.

Within this great majority Niebuhr distinguished three different ways of maintaining the relation between Christ and culture in creative tension. "Christ above Culture" holds the two together in a hierarchical *synthesis* of the realms of the spiritual and the physical.[18] The kingdom of God and the kingdoms of men are complementary—the one sanctifying the other and receiving support in return.

A second mediating motif, "Christ and Culture in Paradox," relates the two *dualistically* by marking off life under God's mercy and life under God's wrath.[19] Believer and unbeliever alike live under law and judgment within culture since only divine restraint of human sinfulness makes cultural life possible. But the believer simultaneously lives in another order— the spiritual order of God's grace where law has no place because sin's power is broken. The believer's dual citizenship imposes two distinct moralities though both are exercised under the one God.

Finally, Niebuhr developed a third motif at work in mainstream Christianity's efforts to hold Christ and culture in creative tension.[20] *Conversion,* appropriately labeled by Niebuhr "Christ the Transformer of Culture," locates the world of man within the world of God even though the human world is fallen and corrupt. As such, the whole creation (natural and human, personal and social) remains open to transformation through the restraining and renewing presence of God in all things and events.

Although offered as a historical typology of Christian ethics, *Christ and Culture* in fact confirmed Niebuhr's arrival at a viable moral stance. The structure and substance of this book leaves little doubt, even to the reader not informed by Niebuhr's other writings, that his sympathies lie with the conversionists. This preference is suggested by Niebuhr's wholly positive presentation and assessment of the "Christ transforming Culture" motif, in contrast to his mixed reviews of the other types examined. As noted above, he found serious and substantive theological and ethical shortcomings in both the excluders ("Christ against Culture") and the accommodators ("Christ of Culture"). His strictures against the synthesists and the dualists were less categorical but no less obvious. He found the static syntheses of "Christ above Culture" too frequently falling victim to institutionalized religion and cultural conservatism, and the unrelieved dualisms of "Christ and Culture in Paradox" too readily fragmenting life into an unalloyed mix of tragedy and joy, of demand and gift. Only the chapter on "Christ the Transformer of Culture" closed without a catalog of questions and criticisms directed against the moral stance under review. This silence, like an artist's signature, tokened Niebuhr's identification with the conversionists.

This silence should not be taken to mean that Niebuhr regarded conversionism as beyond criticism, as fully succeeding where all other positions failed to maintain the proper tension between Christ and culture. In a final chapter which he entitled "A Concluding Unscientific Postscript," Niebuhr made it clear that his fivefold typology was only one way "to seine the sea of history" and that perhaps other typologies (more or less complex) could be employed with more fruitful results. Be that as it may, he was convinced that *no* amount of historical research or systematic reflection would yield a definitive solution to the problem of Christ and culture. The relativities of all things human and the mysteries of all things divine are too great to ever permit any one solution to become *the* Christian answer. That answer must be sought again and again in every particular context and time by finite men responding to the absolute God.

Having disavowed the search for *the* Christian answer, Niebuhr nevertheless found conversionism more adequate and comprehensive than the other solutions. Further evidence of this judgment can be seen in Niebuhr's style of presenting "Christ Transforming Culture" by playing this motif off against the others. The impression gained thereby is the sense that this position includes the strengths and avoids the weaknesses of the others.

Similar and more telling evidence of Niebuhr's sympathies can be discerned in the final chapter where he pointed the way beyond ethical reflection to moral action, beyond typical cases to existential situations. There he portrayed the existential context of moral decision in terms fully consonant with conversionism. He located the choosing self in a historically and socially relative context that is saved from sheer relativity by the presence of the absolute God. This God, known in and through Christ, continually stretches and shatters, corrects and completes all piecemeal human efforts to know and to do the good— a good that finally and fully is nothing less than the kingdoms of this world become the kingdom of God.

In short, Niebuhr's historical reading and personal rendering of the conversionist position seems to take up the dominant concerns and contributions of the other positions—the excluder's reach for heaven and the accommodator's devotion to earth, the synthesist's certainty of sanctity and the dualist's struggle with sin. Precisely this power to include what other positions *affirm* without being bound by their negations was for Niebuhr a strong indication of a position's superior adequacy and comprehensiveness over its competitors. Viewed in this light, *Christ and Culture* was in its entirety a subtle delineation of Niebuhr's emergent ethical stance in somewhat the same way that *The Kingdom of God in America* was an indirect exposition of his emergent theology. In both studies, the history of an idea led to a new grasp of the idea's reality within history.

CONCLUSION: CALL TO PERMANENT REFORMATION

In conclusion, we have noted how Niebuhr's thinking, although seldom explicitly autobiographical, is deeply rooted in his German-American heritage and his own struggle of faith. That dual heritage early gave rise to a binocular view of things that later became a distinctive style of theological and ethical reflection—a synoptic vision that respected the multiformity and individuality of men and movements and yet sought new ways to combine their diverse strengths and to avoid their weaknesses. Underlying that richly dialectical intellect, more was at work than a scholar's curiosity. Niebuhr was a thinker of earnest heart as well as agile mind. His reflective work paralleled and mirrored his life. Both were a continuing search for the meaning of the lordship of God over all of life—joyous and sorrowful, personal and social, Christian and non-Christian, religious and cultural.

We have also traced how Niebuhr's distinctive style and seriousness has produced a brand new whole in theology and ethics. Drawing from incommensurate theological and ethical traditions, Niebuhr's developing thought brought together the theocentric and anthropocentric, the other-worldly and this-worldly in a powerful new vision of Christian thought and life. His "theocentric relativism," so distinctively modern yet thoroughly biblical, brought together the Kingdom of God and the kingdoms of men in unbroken and unconfused union.

This envisioned union is from God's side a continual process of judgment and redemption, from man's side an unending response of repentance and renewal. In short, Niebuhr's new whole in theology and ethics, like the pilgrimage of his personal life, embodied the single imperative required of sinful men by a sovereign God—*permanent reformation!* We must now examine in far greater care and detail Niebuhr's contribution to the ongoing reformation of theology and ethics.

Part Two

NIEBUHR AS THEOLOGIAN

IV. The Theological Standpoint

THE RELATION OF THEOLOGY AND ETHICS

H. Richard Niebuhr can best be described as a moral theologian. There is a balanced reciprocity and symmetry of the theological and the ethical in his thought. His theological work is directed primarily toward the solution of problems confronting the moral life. His ethical reflection is devoted to drawing out the moral implications of the religious life. In other words, theology and ethics are two sides of a single reflective task of understanding faith as an interactional field of relationships between the self, the neighbor and God. Niebuhr's reflective efforts are devoted largely to clarifying that ultimate context in terms of how the God at its center is active in the world and appropriated in experience. He is like Spinoza a "God-intoxicated" thinker. But such clarification serves not only to increase the faithful's understanding of love of God but to illumine and guide their understanding and love of neighbor. Thus Niebuhr weaves theology and ethics together as the warp and woof of his thought. His theological reflection is ethically oriented and his ethical reflection is theologically grounded.

Though theological and ethical reflection are inseparable in Niebuhr's thought, they are not identical. He does not completely reduce theology to ethics or absorb ethics in theology. He insists upon a distinction between theology and ethics because of the distinction between man's relationship to God and his relationship to neighbor. Of course either one of these relationships is subject to distortion and hence can be marked out for concentrated analysis and reformulation. But the distortion of one inevitably mirrors a distortion in the other. These distortions are almost always theological at base for the simple reason that man's relationship to God is determinative of his relationship to neighbor. Thus for Niebuhr theological reflection has a certain priority in the work of the moral theologian. We have seen this priority at work in his developing thought. He traced the ethical failure of the church to the inadequacies of the reigning theologies of his day and set about to lay new theological foundations for ethical action. In the following chapters we shall see that the priority of theology persists in his developed thought as well. For Niebuhr the fundamental task of the Christian moralist is the theological clarification and criticism of believing experience.

Accordingly, our study of Niebuhr's mature thought will begin with his theological program. As we have seen, Niebuhr sought a theology that would combine the radical sovereignty of God and the radical historicity of men. Only such a theology could do justice to historic Christianity and modern existence. Niebuhr's search for this new theological synthesis led him to a recovery and restatement of the meaning of revelation for Christian life and thought. That theology of revelation will be our concern in Part Two. Chapter IV will give a generalized account of the theological standpoint by way of showing that every theological interpretation of believing experience is relative to a particular standpoint in history and faith. Chapters V and VI will detail the full structure and substance of Niebuhr's theology, showing how God is revealed in history and is present to faith.

THEOLOGY AND THE MODERN MIND

Niebuhr's call for a theology of revelation is in no sense a return to Orthodox supernaturalism or biblicism.[1] These long-held conceptions of theological work are no longer possible or even necessary according to Niebuhr. A hundred and fifty years of biblical criticism, historical research and scientific challenge cannot be ignored or repealed. The supernaturalist and biblicist approaches are simply closed to those who desire a fully contemporary as well as consistently Christian faith and theology.

Relinquishing such claims to direct access and absolute certitude in matters of faith is demanded by a profound shift that has taken place in the way modern man understands himself and his world. This shift is a move away from all supernatural explanations and absolute standpoints.[2] Modern man no longer expects or accepts miraculous happenings or indubitable truths. Instead, men of the modern world seek and find understanding *in* the texture of things—in their depth dimensions, their inherent capacities, and their significant interactions. Furthermore, men of the modern world are learning to act on less than perfect and complete understanding of themselves and their world because they have learned that they always see things from a limited point of view in their own history and culture. Thus theological work done in the modern context and spirit is restricted to searching out the presence of God to human experience from a particular standpoint within human experience.

Of course, liberal theology has led the way in adjusting to this secularizing and relativizing of modern life and thought. Liberalism has readily come to terms with secularism's critique of traditional Christianity's other-worldliness. It claims with some justification that its conception of God as personal presence and power *within* nature, history and consciousness actually has more affinity with biblical religion and personal faith than do the orthodox conceptions of God as supernaturally beyond and other than the world. But liberalism's ability and willingness to come to terms with relativism have been far less successful. It has willingly surrendered traditional Christianity's exclusivism and recognized the presence and truth of God in other religions. But liberalism has typically maintained that Christianity contains the highest or the final truth about God. In fact, liberal theology has virtually identified God with the highest values and achievements of Christian culture.

As we have seen, Niebuhr credited the downfall of liberal theology to this failure to accept the full implications of relocating God within personal and social experience. All empirically based theologies are limited to a particular and hence relative standpoint in history and faith.[3] Far from proving a disadvantage to theology, such an admission is demanded by proper recognition of the sovereignty of God as well as by acknowledgment of the historicity of man. The truth about God and man cannot be consistently maintained or intelligibly related unless the historical and religious relativism of every theological standpoint is accepted.

Historical Relativism

Theologians and moralists are not the only ones who have been discomfited by the realization that all experience and knowledge are conditioned by one's standpoint. Comparative studies in history, anthropology and sociology have established beyond reasonable doubt that human beings are historical selves whose metaphysics, logic, theology and ethics, like their sciences, economics, politics and rhetoric are limited, moving and changing in time.[4] But the secular disciplines have adjusted to this realization faster than their sacred counterparts. The natural and social sciences, the formal disciplines of logic and mathematics, the literary and fine arts and even some recent philosophy have learned to do their work in the confidence that their finite perspectives, imperfect achievements and tentative agreements are grounded in a reality which they know in part if not *in toto*. They have learned to think and act without benefit of universal categories of thought and universal consensus of beliefs.

Niebuhr believes such confidence in probable knowledge and tentative commitment is fully justifiable. Historical relativism can be accepted without collapsing into skepticism (judging every viewpoint to be totally unreliable) or subjectivism (claiming that every viewpoint is equally viable):

> It is not evident that the man who is forced to confess that his view of things is conditioned by the standpoint he occupies must doubt the reality of what he sees. It is not apparent that one who knows that his concepts are not universal must also doubt that they are concepts of the universal, or that one who understands how all experience is historically mediated must believe that nothing is mediated through history.[5]

Niebuhr ties this confidence to two "givens" present in all historically relative experience. One barrier against skepticism or subjectivism is the independently existing "objects" of our perceptions and valuations. Though these objects appear to us through time-conditioned and culture-variant categories, they are *there* in their own right, independent of all human thinking, wishing or feeling.

The second protection against the dangers of sheer relativity is the social character of every point of view. Each individual occupies what is in fact a standpoint formed and informed by a society of companions. His personal experience is thereby always "subject to the test of experience on the part of companions who look from the same standpoint in the same direction as well as to the test of consistency with the principles and concepts that have grown out of past experience in the same community." [6] For Niebuhr, the possibility of confronting the objects of experience personally and communicating about them socially furnishes adequate grounds for the discovery of reliable knowledge in a relative world.

Given this general realistic and social theory of knowledge, Niebuhr declares that theology must face the problems and make the adjustments required by historical relativism:

> There does not seem then to be any apparent possibility of escape from the dilemma of historical relativism for any type of

theology. The historical point of view of the observer must be taken into consideration in every case since no observer can get out of history into a realm beyond time-space; if reason is to operate at all it must be content to work as an historical reason.[7]

Dangers of skepticism and temptations toward subjectivism will dog this situation, but Niebuhr is confident that these pitfalls can be avoided. Individual religious standpoints are clustered together in a community of religious experience and interpretation. Within this community, the individual's experience and understanding are subject to correction and corroboration by the entire community of believers, past and present. More important, the independently existing religious Object stands over against all our finite and conditioned apprehensions—always resisting, always renewing, yet always responding to those apprehensions. Stressing the independent reality of the God experienced and the communal nature of that experience, Niebuhr sees a way for believers and theologians to live with historical relativism without succumbing to a despairing skepticism or a deceptive subjectivism.

This attention to the objective content and social context of all historical experience uncovers a second way for Niebuhr in which all theological standpoints are relative. Theology always takes place in a particular community that experiences God in a particular way. As such, theology seeks to clarify and commend the community's experience *of that God*. Theology's ultimate task is not simply cataloging the beliefs and practices of a given historic community. Rather, theological reflection aims at deepening that community's understanding and response to the God in its midst. Thus theological work is always relative to a particular religious as well as historical standpoint.

Religious Relativism

Theological reflection begins and ends with faith. This faith, according to Niebuhr, is not a matter of believing an inspired text (biblicism) or of affirming an authoritative doctrine (orthodoxy). Rather, faith is a dynamic structure of interpersonal relationships that center in God and permeate all personal and social activities.[8] For the Christian, this interactional field embraces the entire universe, since the God at its center is ubiquitously sovereign. But Niebuhr maintains that Christian faith, though centering in a God universally present in nature and history, is *not* a faith universally available in nature or history. Christian faith has emerged from and is embodied in a particular historic community. Christian theology, then, must always reflect faith's communal and historic character:

> Being in social history it cannot be a personal and private theology nor can it live in some non-churchly sphere of political and cultural history; its home is the church; its language is the language of the church; and with the church it is directed toward the universal from which the church knows itself to derive its being and to which it points in all its faith and works.[9]

Theological reflection always speaks *from* historic faith *to* historic faith.

Working under the constraints of historic faith, Niebuhr insists that theology can only be "confessional." [10] A confessional style of theology is no exercise in telling "what Jesus means to me" without critically comparing that meaning alongside the experiences of others both inside *and* outside the church. Theology done in a confessional way critically evaluates Christian life and thought in the light of faith's Object. It also critically engages non-Christian perspectives on human experience by searching out their internal weakness and offering constructive alternatives. But confessional theology always addresses the church and the world without claiming finality or universality for its formulations of the Christian faith. It offers to believer and unbeliever alike a limited vision of an unlimited God.

Niebuhr argues that theology done in a confessional way operates under a double constraint. The confessional approach is not only ' demanded by the *historical* limitations of a given theology's standpoint. It is also a tacit acknowledgment of the *sinfulness* of those who occupy that standpoint.[11] A theology based on historic revelation is as much a confession of sin as a confession of faith. Theologies which refuse the confessional approach add self-congratulation and self-defensiveness to their own inherent imperfections. Such aggressive pride and protectiveness have no place in a "sinner's theology" which at best can only explain how the Christian community reasons about things and what it sees from its limited point of view in historic faith.

Niebuhr aptly summarizes the ways men respond to the discovery of their own historical and religious relativity:

> In the presence of their relativities men seem to have three possibilities: they can become nihilists and consistent skeptics, who affirm that nothing can be relied upon; or they can flee to the authority of some relative position, affirming that a church or a philosophy or a value like that of life for the self, is absolute; or they can accept their relativities with faith in the infinite Absolute to whom all their relative views, values and duties are subject. In the last case they can make their confessions and decisions both with confidence and with the humility which accepts completion and correction and even conflict from and with others who stand in the same relation to the Absolute. They will then in their fragmentary knowledge be able to state with conviction what they have seen and heard, the truth for them; but they will not contend that it is the whole truth and nothing but the truth, and they will not become dogmatists unwilling to seek out what other men have seen and heard of that same Object they have fragmentarily known.[12]

Obviously siding with the latter alternative, Niebuhr develops a theology which he has appropriately called "theocentric relativism."[13]

NIEBUHR'S THEOCENTRIC RELATIVISM

What does Niebuhr see from his vantage point and how does he see it? What does he confess from where he stands? Niebuhr's theology is neither an explication of God in himself nor a description of man's response to God. "What is known and knowable in theology is God in relation to self and to neighbor, and self and neighbor in relation to God." [14] Theological discourse about the objective reality of God must not be separated from discourse about the subjective experience of faith. Such separations have, of course, typified powerful theologies in the past—notably Protestant orthodoxy's devotion to the objective side of theological inquiry and Protestant liberalism's concentration on the subjective element. These separations have continued into the contemporary period in such original restatements as Barth's christologic objectivism and Bultmann's existential subjectivism. But Niebuhr contends that theology must hold these two aspects of religious experience together and bring them to mutual clarity. "Theology must attend to the God of faith if it is to understand faith no less than it must attend to faith in God if it is to understand God." [15]

Then where and how does this "complex object" come to appearance for Niebuhr's theology? What are the sources and the norms by which Niebuhr speaks of God and the world in continuous interaction? As noted above, Niebuhr is convinced that the direct appeals to nature, scripture or intuition which were so typical of earlier theologies are no longer possible. Christian theology cannot point to nature, saying that what it means by God and his will can be known if only men will look together at stars and trees and flowers. Nor can it point to scripture, saying that what it means by God and his will can be known if only men will read what is there written. Nor can Christian theology point to inwardness, declaring that God's voice can be heard in moral consciousness or numinous awareness. Read in different contexts, the "books" of nature, scripture and inwardness will mean different things. For Christian theology, these three are sources of theological understanding only when they are interpreted from the Christian standpoint in history and in faith.[16]

If theological reflection cannot appeal directly to nature, scripture or inwardness, from whence does it speak? Niebuhr's answer is clear but by no means simple:

Christian theology must begin today with *revelation* because it knows that men cannot think about God save as historic, com-

munal beings and save as believers. It must ask what revelation
means for Christians rather than what it ought to mean for all
men, everywhere and at all times. And it can pursue its inquiry
only by recalling the story of Christian life and by analyzing
what Christians see from their limited point of view in history
and faith.[17]

Embedded in this straightforward appeal to revelation is a
highly complex understanding of precisely what revelation
means and how revelation happens in human experience. Un-
packing that complex understanding involves nothing less than
explicating the entire formal and material content of Niebuhr's
theology. Everything of theological importance that Niebuhr
has to say can be found in his understanding of the revelation
of "God for man" and "man before God" which is given in
Christian history and to Christian faith.

V. Revelation and History

Although Niebuhr asserts that theology begins with revelation, he believes that, given the modern world's scientific and relativistic self-understanding, talk about revelation can only make sense if revelation is truly *historical* in three distinct but connected senses of that term. First, revelation must mean that a decisive disclosure of God in and through ordinary events has occurred in our past histories. Second, revelation must mean that this past disclosure can bring about a similar disclosure of God in and through ordinary events in our present histories. Finally, revelation must mean that this past disclosure is mediated to present experience in and through ordinary historical channels. For Niebuhr only a revelation that is fully historical will prove believable and relevant to men who must live and die in history.

But this demand for revelation's full historicity raises a whole nest of formal problems. How can revelation mean both history and God? How can ordinary historical events and relationships, whether past or present contain the reality of God and the meaning of life? How can God and his will be mediated through events which can be studied and explained, at least on one level, like all historical events? Moreover, how can revelation be both past event and present experience? If revelation means God and his will mediated through certain historical events, is not faith reduced to believing certain things about special events in the past? Does not revelation become a static "then and there" instead of a dynamic "here and now"?

Niebuhr addresses these problems in his "two-aspect theory of history." [1] The problems of revelation and history require a distinction between "internal history" and "external history." These terms are used somewhat equivocally in Niebuhr's writings. Sometimes the distinction between internal and external marks different *ontological dimensions* of historical events— different dimensions of being and value in human happenings. At other times, these terms denote distinctive *epistemic modes* of historical understanding—different ways of perceiving the nature and meaning of human occurrences. But both uses taken together furnish Niebuhr a way of locating revelation in history and transmitting revelation through history.

THE HISTORICAL LOCUS OF REVELATION

Niebuhr's two-aspect theory of history grows out of his conviction that all experience and understanding are conditioned by one's point of view.[2] The relativity of both historical subjects and objects means that differing perspectives yield differing experiences and conceptualizations of reality. Two perspectives from widely different cultural and historical standpoints will obviously differ. But even within a broadly shared viewpoint certain kinds of experiences or levels of reality are not automatically available to all members of that cultural history. Every culture contains an immense number of communities committed to their own distinctive views of reality and morality. Such distinctive views are not available or intelligible from an *external* perspective. Only a perspective *internal* to a given community can apprehend that community's thought and life.

Thus for Niebuhr "external history" refers to those aspects of experience and reality which are available to anyone sharing a culture-wide stance in nature and society. Such aspects include all occurrences and entities which are perceivable to the senses and explainable in terms of physical, biological, psychological,

and sociological forces and functions. "Internal history" denotes those aspects of experience and reality which can be apprehended only through participation in the theoretical and
practical life of a distinctive community. Such aspects include
metaphysical unities, ethical values, spiritual meanings, and
personal encounters which are discoverable through personal
interaction and explainable by means of the distinctive language
and logic of that community.

While clearly distinguishing these two histories, Niebuhr
seeks to preserve their "duality in union." His distinction is not
a division of history into two kinds of reality on the same plane,
each kind apprehensible from the same standpoint by the same
cognitive faculties (orthodoxy's miraculous events in history).
Nor is this a division of history into two orders of reality on two
different planes, each order perceivable from the respective
standpoints of totally different cognitive faculties (neoorthodoxy's saving events in history). The distinction between external history and internal history expresses Niebuhr's conviction
that the *same* historical reality may be seen in *different* aspects
from *distinctive* standpoints. Thus Niebuhr's double-aspect theory views revelation as, simultaneously, ordinary occurrence
(perceivable and explainable like any natural occurrence) and
religious event (apprehensible and understandable as a special
divine event).[3]

In this duality in union, Niebuhr takes a somewhat Kantian
approach to revelation and history.[4] Like Kant, he distin-
guishes external history as the sphere of pure reason and internal history as the domain of practical reason. Morever, like
Kant, Niebuhr locates revelation within value experiences interpreted by practical reasoning rather than in factual data
analyzed by theoretical reasoning. But Niebuhr avoids a Kantian separation of experience into dichotomous realms of being
(facts versus values) or autonomous modes of knowing (reason
versus faith) by modifying him in two crucial ways.

Niebuhr overcomes Kant's separation of pure and practical
reasoning, in part, by reconceiving them as distinctive functions
of an integral rational *imagination*.[5] Both pure and practical
reasoning work on the "brute data" given in experience by

"imaging" and "imagining" beyond the data. The immediate data of pure reasoning are "sensations of the body" (visual and auditory, tactile and kinesthetic, etc.), while those of practical reasoning are "affections of the self" (joys and sorrows, loves and hates, fears and hopes, etc.). Rational imagination supplies what is lacking in the immediate data by furnishing patterns and paradigms of understanding and action, of interpretation and response. Thus, for Niebuhr, pure and practical reasoning differ primarily in the *kinds* of images used and knowledge sought in reasoning from a concrete standpoint.[6] *Pure* reasoning deals with the entire physical, biological, psychological, socio- logical and rational complex in which an event occurs. It de- scribes cause-effect relations as well as novel manifestations of general tendencies and capacities. Its patterns and paradigms are impersonal, effectual and descriptive.[7] *Practical* reasoning deals with the unities, values, meanings and encounters in an event apprehended through faith. Its images are personal, valu- ational and dramatic.[8] In either case, the knowledge gained is an imaginative construct built upon the sensory and affective clues of immediate experience.

Niebuhr further modifies Kant in an equally radical way by stressing the historical relativity of all reasoning.[9] Pure and practical reasoning not only work on data which are historically given but are themselves historically conditioned. This condi- tioning occurs by way of the effect of language on reasoning and of the role of companions on understanding. Reason interprets the data of experience (sensations and affections) through pat- terns, images, and models. But these conceptual-linguistic forms are always drawn from and employed within a particular social context.[10] Individual views of reality arise out of a process of communication, correction, and corroboration from other indi- viduals who share a similar perspective.[11] Therefore, man sees, thinks, understands and believes only as a self *in* a particular history and *with* a particular history.[12]

Finally, then, Niebuhr locates revelation in the complex of internal history. Not all inner history is revelatory of God, self and neighbor, but in principle any historical event can be revelatory if God and his will are apprehended in that event internally through faithful reasoning. In such cases, practical reasoning employs imaginative models and metaphors which are drawn from and confirmed within a committed community. Therefore, revelation is always located in past and present internal history. Revelation denotes those events in the past which furnish the images and create the community through which God and his will are apprehended within present historical experience.

Thus far Niebuhr's analysis of external and internal history shows how revelation can mean both history and God without confusing or separating them. This way of putting it is reminiscent of the classical christological definition of Chalcedon. Indeed, in anticipation of further discussion below, we may note here that Niebuhr's two-aspect theory of history is a highly original restatement of the Chalcedonian requirement that all talk about the human and the divine in Jesus Christ must maintain the duality in union of these two natures "without confusion, change, separation, or division." Of course, unlike classical christologies, Niebuhr does not see a uniquely supernatural joining of God and man in the Christ event. But, by transposing the creed's static language of two "natures" into the dynamic language of two "histories," Niebuhr finds within the ancient formula a statement of the lasting truth about man's relation to God and God's relation to man in history. The duality in union of God and man in the *Christ* event is the paradigmatic way that God and man are related in *every* event.

But this account of Niebuhr's two-aspect theory of history only partially illumines the remaining problem of how revelation can mean past event and present reality. Further attention must now be given to how revelation as past event is historically mediated to present experience.

THE HISTORICAL TRANSMISSION OF REVELATION

Niebuhr rejects outright a number of typical solutions to the problem of how a past event can be appropriated in the present as a means of revelation. Contrary to claims by certain expressions of orthodox and liberal theology, he rules out objective historical research as a bridge between a past revelatory event and a present revelatory experience.[13] Historical research can explain the external aspects of such an event by reconstructing its cause-effect relationships within its cultural, geographical, economic, and political context. It can delineate the novelty of that event by describing the ways the event actualized certain potentialities and tendencies in human nature and society. But finally, historical research can do no more than record the distinctive but by no means unique fact that a certain people have attached great religious significance to that event and show how this devotion influenced cultural, economic, and political developments in subsequent history. Such historical investigation and explanation, though valid and important in its own right, establishes no *religious* knowledge of that revelatory event.[14]

Niebuhr also rejects liberal theology's value methods and neoorthodoxy's dualistic historiography as ways of linking past event and present experience in revelation. Each of these approaches claims to be a *historical* way of joining past revelation to present experience quite apart from scholarly historical research. Nineteenth-century liberalism typically appeals to some set of "eternal values" as both the means and the criteria for historically extrapolating an event's revelatory and timeless value. Twentieth-century neoorthodoxy invokes a distinctive access to the past which immediately apprehends a revelatory event's inner or spiritual meaning. Though Niebuhr learned and appropriated much from each of these approaches, and though his language bears more than superficial similarity to both, his fully elaborated two-aspect theory of history and revelation neither duplicates nor combines these methods. Niebuhr found a common failing in liberalism's value methods and neoorthodoxy's pneumatic exegesis. Both of these proffered solutions to the problem of how revelation can be a past event and a present reality balk at working within the theological limitations of a fully historical standpoint. Liberalism's claim to discover revelation in history by use of values that are not themselves given through history ("eternal truths in changing categories") and neoorthodoxy's claim of privileged access to certain historical events through the special reading of a special book about those events ("the Word speaking through the words") are both denials of the *radical* historicity of revelation and faith.

Put briefly, for Niebuhr a past event can be a means of revelation in the present when its revelatory internal aspects are mediated through a historic community that embodies these aspects in communal monuments *and* living selves. Niebuhr calls this complex process "historical memory." [15] Despite its importance to his thought, he nowhere presents a full and systematic account of this process of remembering the revelatory past in and for the revelatory present. But the main lines of this distinctive mode of historical cognition can be constructed from Niebuhr's writings.

The requirement for knowing any event in the past in any of its aspects is remembering it. By emphasizing this obvious fact, Niebuhr calls attention to the creative and critical participation required for all knowledge of the past. No event of the past can be known from a point of view wholly neutral or alien to it. Some common ground of relationship and interest must exist between the remembering knower and the remembered event. The nature of this common ground depends upon the kind of historical cognition intended. In order to reconstruct external aspects of an event, one must share some common ground psychologically, sociologically and culturally with that past event.[16] In order to remember an event as revelatory, one must participate in the communal history and faith which originally knew it as revelatory.

The possibility of such participation, in Niebuhr's understanding, involves a certain view of time and community.[17] For the participant in a communal history and faith, time is not serial. Time is not a chronological series in which past events are dead and gone, and future happenings are beyond consideration and influence. Rather, time is durational.

> What is past is not gone; it abides in memory; what is future is not non-existent but present to us as our potentiality. Time here is organic, or it is social, so that past and future associate

with each other in the present. Time in our history is not another
dimension of the external space world in which we live, but a
dimension of our life and of our community's being. We are not
in this time but it is in us.[18]

Time for Niebuhr is an enduring internal aspect of personal and
communal existence whereby the present is dependent upon the
past held in memory and upon the future held in anticipation.

But the possibility of holding the past in memory and the
future in anticipation through succeeding generations depends
upon the organic relation of the personal and the social within
a communal history and faith.[19] The past and the future endure
in selves. When selves hold meanings in common which have
grown out of shared events, they are bound together in community. Within this community of selves, these founding and
shared meanings may endure through successive generations far
beyond the events and the persons who originally constituted the
community, if they are continually embodied in the stories and
lives that make up the community. So long as the community
continues to tell "the story of its life" in word and deed to each
new generation, these shared meanings are mediated to later
participants in the community.

In this way, Niebuhr shows how a revelatory event in the past
can be *historically* communicated to the present through the
living memory of a historic community. But how does such an
enduring community distinguish between its present remembering and its remembered past? What prevents the community
from losing, in its own remembering, those meanings which
initiated its history and faith as a community?

Niebuhr meets this problem by stressing the importance of
the objective embodiments of the original community's memory
and of their critical reinterpretation in the enduring community's remembering.[20] Put another way, a past revelatory event
is mediated to the present through communal *monuments* (symbols, rituals, documents) which objectively embody those meanings out of the past, and by living *persons* (believers, teachers,
theologians) who critically appropriate this legacy in the pres-

ent. Thus Niebuhr accounts for the integrity and continuity of the religious community's memory without relying on the earlier theories of biblical supernaturalism (which free memory of the past from any dependence upon the enduring historic community or the critical reinterpretations of men) or on newer theories of collective unconsciousness (which hold the past in memory without recourse to the memories of individual participants in the community).

The importance of communal monuments and contemporary interpreters for preserving the integrity of the remembered revelation deserves further explanation because it involves Niebuhr's view of scripture, liturgy and tradition. Religious communities typically express those revelatory events which gave rise to their history and faith in certain sacred writings and rituals. Though these communal monuments are not themselves revelatory, they are an indispensable means for the communal mediation of the revelatory past to subsequent generations in the community.

> Without the Bible and the rites of the institutional church the inner history of the Christian community could not continue, however impossible it is to identify the memory of that community with the documents. Though we cannot point to what we mean by revelation by directing attention to the historic facts as embodied and as regarded from without, we can have no continuing inner history through which to point without embodiment. "Words without thoughts never to heaven go" but thoughts without words never remain on earth. Moreover, such is the alternation of our life that the thought which becomes word can become thought again only through the mediation of the word; the word which becomes flesh can become word for us again only through the flesh.[21]

For Niebuhr a community's monuments (documents and rites) are the "permanent possibilities" by which the present-day community remembers past revelatory events as revelatory. But they remain only possibilities until their inner meanings are properly interpreted and personally appropriated within the community. These documents and rituals can and will be

understood differently in different contexts, from different standpoints. Thus, these linguistic and dramatic forms are carriers of
revelation only so long as they are understood and internalized
in a community of selves who share the same internal history
out of which they originally came.[22]

For this reason Niebuhr recognizes an indispensable relation
between a community's *tradition* and its scriptures and litur-
gies.[23] His approach to the nature and function of tradition
grows out of his understanding of the historical and social character of all experience. Unlike the understanding of tradition
within Catholic and Protestant scholasticism, tradition for Niebuhr is not a rigid structure of social organization, doctrinal
formulation or liturgical observation impervious to change. Tradition is the "dynamic structure of modifiable habits" necessary
for all human existence. It is a living social process "constantly
changing, constantly in need of criticism, but constant also as
the continuing memory, value system and habit structure of a
society." For the Christian community, the Bible and the sacraments are the primary mediators of tradition. These "primary
documents" contain the logic and language through which the
primitive community apprehended and organized its experience
under the impact of the revelatory event. But the Christian community's continuing memory, value system and habit structure
are also mediated through the critical reinterpretation of the
Bible and the sacraments, in word and deed, by contemporary
participants in the Christian community. Present-day social and
personal experience, scientific and philosophical understanding
require the church to ask new questions of the Bible and the
sacraments and to read their familiar communications in new
settings.[24] Through this constant rethinking and re-searching of
its living memory for appropriate patterns and models, the
Christian community maintains a genuine dialogue with and
dependence on the revelatory event.

Perhaps the question about the fidelity of the community's
remembering still persists, despite this fuller description of Niebuhr's position. Indeed, are there ever finally any guarantees
that the church at some time or place has not and will not mis-

construe the meaning of revelation, especially since every fresh appropriation is a work of finite and sinful men? Niebuhr can only answer "no" to such persistent questioning. There are no such *ultimate* guarantees—only the confidence finally that God resists the error and consents to the truth of our apprehensions of revelation in our own time and place. But Niebuhr does see two *penultimate* checks against all the miscarriages of communal memory, whether these failures are a consequence of finitude or perversity.

One such check is the sheer "givenness" of the scriptural embodiments of revelation. Niebuhr acknowledges a variety of memories of the revelatory event within the scriptures themselves, to say nothing of the community's traditions. "But there always remain the original portraits by which all later pictures may be compared and by which all caricatures may be corrected." [25]

A second proximate check against radical failure or innovation in remembering the revelatory event is the correction and corroboration offered by the *whole* church, past and present, near and far.[26] For Niebuhr the meaning of revelation lies less with any individual, party or group within the church than with the whole community of believers and knowers—dynamic and complementary, diverse and contradictory as they are. This church serves as a "society for the mutual extraction of motes and beams." [27] Every particular reappropriation of the revelatory event should be undertaken in ecumenical dialogue and tested for correction or corroboration against all those who share and speak of this revelation.

Finally, then, Niebuhr believes that appeals to scriptural priority and to ecumenical dialogue are powerful and persistent checks against bald distortions of the meaning of revelation. But ultimately the continuity and fidelity between the primitive and contemporary experience of revelation rests in the God known in and through that revelation.

Despite warnings at the outset that as a theologian Niebuhr is primarily concerned with methodological problems, his theology as described thus far may seem oppressively abstract and gen-

eral. Doubtless, any such impressions are partly the consequence of the retelling here which, by necessity, has compressed
and systematized a wide variety of his materials on the subject.
Notwithstanding, Niebuhr's analysis of revelation and history *is*
highly formal. Though he obviously works with Christian revelation in mind, he intends to illumine how any community with
a distinctive history and faith arises and endures. But fortu-
nately Niebuhr's reflections on revelation are not limited to
solving formal problems of revelation and history. He does
write concretely and passionately about Christian revelation and
Christian faith. His views are nowhere systematically developed, but a careful reading and constructive rearrangement of
his materials disclose an eloquent understanding of God, self
and neighbor as these are revealed to Christian faith.

VI. Revelation and Faith

For Niebuhr, the Christian community derives its life and thought about God, self and neighbor from the event of Jesus Christ. But he sees more at work here than a sociological necessity or a pedagogical advantage for the Christian community to give expression to its faith through images and stories of a concrete personage.

Of course, like the central figures or cultic heroes in other world religions, Jesus Christ does play such roles in the Christian community. Niebuhr's historical and sociological studies of religion under the inspiration of Ernst Troeltsch helped him to appreciate and understand how, from a strictly human standpoint, verbal and liturgical portrayals of Jesus Christ preserve the identity of the Christian community through changing times and places.[1] His work on the importance of symbolic language under the tutelage of Ernst Cassirer and Stephen Pepper sensitized him to the way in which the life, death and resurrection of Jesus Christ has served as *the* great parable for interpreting the whole of human history and natural process in Christian thought and life.[2]

Thus Niebuhr readily admits that Jesus Christ is the symbolic center of the church's communal life and religious understanding. But he maintains that the Christian community appeals to Jesus Christ in its history and faith for reasons that go beyond the pragmatic effectiveness and social utility of stories about him. Christian faith appeals to the events surrounding Jesus Christ because those events *called* and *call* forth a new understanding of human existence and a new order of personal relationships under God by transforming "natural faith" into "radical faith." [3]

THE PATHOLOGY OF NATURAL FAITH

Examining and describing human life in its most typical manifestations and general structures, Niebuhr contends that faith is given with human life itself:

> Men are so created that they cannot and do not live without faith.[4]
>
> Not only the just but the unjust, insofar as they live, live by faith.[5]
>
> To live is to use standards and to confess in action our faith in the existence of values.[6]
>
> As long as a man lives he must believe in something for the sake of which he lives; without belief in something that makes life worth living man cannot exist.[7]

Some form of faith or another is a *natural* condition and expression of all human existence.

Niebuhr notes that faith is typically described in one of two fundamental ways—faith as a distinctive way of *knowing* and faith as a distinctive structure of *relationships*.[8] For the first set of meanings, faith is generally characterized as either mental assent to saving truths or direct apprehension of ultimate reality. The second set conceives of faith as a structured relationship between persons who are bound together by some source of worth and obligation that transcends them. Niebuhr sees truth in both approaches since faith always involves both knowledge and relationships. But he contends that relationships are more fundamental and comprehensive than beliefs or visions. Therefore, he subordinates faith as a way of knowing to faith as a way of relating. Faith is a structure of interpersonal relationships which is expressed in all man's practical and theoretical activity.

More precisely, Niebuhr defines faith as a *triadic* structure of trust-loyalty relationships.

> In analyzing the structure or nature of faith in this sense we are involved in the examination of a dynamic interpersonal process in which there are not two terms simply, but three—the self, the other, and the cause; and in which there is not one response (that of trust in the faithful, for instance) that maintains the structure, but where two responses are called for, trust and loyalty; and these two responses move in two directions—toward the other and toward the common cause.[9]

Niebuhr often speaks of selected aspects of this dynamic triad and double movement for purposes of emphasis. Thus, for example, sometimes he speaks of the trust-loyalty relationship between two persons.[10] At other times he speaks of the trust-loyalty relationship between a person and his center of value.[11] But Niebuhr always holds these various elements together in a living triad of reciprocal relationships between persons and their shared cause.[12]

All three terms (the self, the other, and the cause) are involved in the phenomenon of faith, but the central or determinative factor is the cause.[13] This "terminal" of faith's triad determines the quality and the scope of relationships within the triad. Although life is always lived amid conflicting and competing causes, one or more of these always become preeminent. As *the* source from which all worth is derived and duty is determined, the preeminent cause functions as the ground of personal and social existence. Expressed in religious terms, these absolutized causes function as god or gods, since they guarantee life's value and determine life's purpose.

We arrive, then, at the problem of deity by setting out from the universal experience of faith, of reliance or trust in something. Luther expressed this idea long ago when he asked "What does it mean to have a God, or what is God?" And answered his question by saying, "Trust and faith of the heart alone make both God and idol. . . . For the two, faith and God, hold together. Whatever then thy heart clings to . . . and relies upon, that is properly thy God." [14]

In short, human life in all of its reflective, affective and active expressions is *religiously* grounded because all men live by faith in some god.

But Niebuhr sees only tragedy in such natural faith, because the causes for which men live in natural faith are finite. These finite gods can never convey infinite value or conscript universal obligation. They can only guarantee meaning to life for a time, and only elicit devotion to causes that fragment life. "Hence," says Niebuhr, "we become aware of two characteristics of our faith and its gods: that we are divided within ourselves and socially by our religion, and that our gods are unable to save us from the ultimate destruction of meaningless existence." [15]

Niebuhr indicates the ways in which faith in false gods fragment personal and social existence in his analysis of two major pathological forms of natural faith—"henotheism" and "polytheism." [16] For henotheistic faith, some social unit (such as family, nation, church, civilization, or even humanity) fulfills the function of god by conveying value to and requiring service of its members. Polytheistic faith depends for its value on many centers of concern (such as health, fame, wealth, pleasure) and divides its loyalties among these many interests.

These two pathological forms of faith, often interchangeable in the lives of selves, ultimately fail to provide personal and social integration. Polytheism is the more diffuse in its effect on personal and social existence, while henotheism is the more demonic.[17] The multiple value centers and scattered loyalties of polytheism obviously fragment life. In polytheistic forms of faith, the self and society become assemblages of activities and associations with no unifying core.

In contrast to such pluralism of self and society, Niebuhr sees henotheistic faith offering a relatively greater unification of self and society. Henotheism arranges competing interests and conflicting duties into a hierarchy according to their ability to enhance the "closed society" which functions as god. But precisely this unification often results in far more destructiveness than polytheistic faiths are capable of producing. By absolutizing some closed society (whether ethnic, political or religious), those who are excluded from the community are treated at best as means to communal ends and at worst as threats to communal survival. Henotheistic faiths have been the occasion for human history's greatest brutalities and aggressions. Moreover, the seeming solidarity of henotheistic faiths is always undermined by intramural and extramural conflicts so that, in fact, henotheisms offer no enduring center for personal and social existence.[18] Thus, for Niebuhr, man's gods, whether pluralistic or social, divide him against himself and estrange him from his fellow creatures.

For Niebuhr, something more fundamental lies behind the failures of the gods of natural religion to give life real integrity and lasting meaning than their own finitude. The inevitable collapse and resultant destructiveness of the gods of natural faith are ultimately manifestations of the judgment of the One and True God.[19] Divine judgment is not limited to some apocalyptic crisis at the end of history or to some eschatological fulfillment beyond the plane of history. Judgment is an ever-present activity of God in the lives of men that comes to appearance in all limitation and conflict, in all suffering and loss. This ever-present judgment is, however, always subservient to redemptive ends. Thus, God continually disrupts those human lives and groups which are centered in the gods of natural faith, at the cost of great suffering to all involved, in order to open them up to the possibility of a radical faith that never divides and never dies.

This means that Niebuhr takes up all human suffering into a fundamentally redemptive context. As noted earlier, the question of God's power and goodness in a world wracked by pain and destructiveness lies near the center of Niebuhr's personal and theological struggles with faith. Indeed, he sees Job's problem at the very heart of all religion. If God is the One, All-determining Power, then why isn't his goodness more evident in a world miserably oppressed? If God is the One, All-encompassing Good, then why isn't his power more effective in a world persistently evil? This age-old dilemma has been variously engaged throughout Christian history.

Unlike his liberal theological predecessors, Niebuhr does not approach this conundrum from the assumption of God's goodness. Although convinced that faith's final assurance is the goodness of God, Niebuhr insists that this confidence must not be won at the price of sentimentalizing or segmenting the power of God—seeing God's hand only in the beneficent and happy experiences of life. The Good God must be found *in* the Powerful God—the God who moves through good *and* evil, through life *and* death to achieve his purposes and to establish his kingdom. For, in Niebuhr's judgment, to place *any* power or good alongside God or even over against God compromises the radical monotheism of radical faith—the singularity and sovereignty of God.

This way of coming at the problem of suffering and evil is clearly reflected in Niebuhr's frequent allusion to Alfred North Whitehead's dictum on religion: "It is the transition from God the void to God the enemy and from God the enemy to God the companion." [20] While Whitehead intended this formula to mark out the stages in religion's evolution, Niebuhr takes this movement as the "experiential logic" of all religion. Every religious quest and community grows out of a sense of radical incompleteness and strangeness at life's core. All natural religions and, indeed, all cultural systems are efforts to fill this Void with lasting substance and meaning. Unhappily, these efforts are finally neither effective nor enduring. Sooner or later they collapse into the Void which they are intended to dispel. Natural religion and cultural existence are cyclic journeys from nothingness into nothingness.

This coming to grief and death of all things human, however, seems due less to an indifferent universe than to a relentless

Enemy. As we experience them, finite lives and loves do not *happen* to die—they are *brought* to death. Life is haunted by the sense of an inimical Power that seems bent on returning all things to the Void from which they came. All natural religions, whatever their personal, social or cultural form, are attempts to escape or to appease this Nemesis, but none successfully dispel "the slow sure doom that falls pitiless and dark" on all things finite and human.

Yet, according to Niebuhr, this grim round is not life's only course and faith's only recourse. There can come into human life a *radical* faith that transforms this cycle of death into a journey to life. Unlike natural religions, radical faith promises no escape or evasion from the Void and the Enemy, but it does re-vision and reinterpret them. Radical faith sees and understands that the Void and the Enemy are one and the same—they are the Companion God who will not let us rest until we rest in him. The Void and the Enemy are but manifestations of an infinite and inclusive Love that breaks down every finite center and circle of love put in its place. These "tutors" goad and guide us into a companionship with God and neighbor that holds no death and no divisions.

Capsuled in this sober but splendid vision is Niebuhr's entire understanding of sin and salvation. Sin is a matter of the *false faith* of natural religion. But the problem with this false faith is not the finitude of the gods of natural religion, as if finite loves and loyalties were somehow inherently evil or opposed to God. Rather, the trouble with natural religion is that it substitutes some finite sense of devotion and duty for what the infinite God alone can provide—an absolute and inclusive cause that consecrates all finite existence. Sin then is not a matter of loving limited goods and serving limited causes. Sin is natural religion's unlimited commitment to limited goods and causes. Correspondingly, salvation is a matter of supplanting the idolatrous and partisan commitments of natural faith with radical faith's singular devotion and duty to God. And, for Niebuhr, this supplanting is clearly a dethroning rather than a destroying of limited goods and causes. Radical faith requires only that all

finite loves and loyalties be brought under subjection and service to their infinite Sum and Source.

Yet something more must be said to get at the bottom of Niebuhr's view of the natural disordering and the radical reorder-
ing of human faith. Why *do* men persist in their devotion to
limited loves and loyalties? Why do men cling so doggedly and
serve so devotedly those human causes which are so obviously
marred by imperfection and marked for death? These questions
go to the root motives and meanings of natural faith—to the
real pathology of natural religion. Finally, Niebuhr argues,
men give themselves to finite concerns and communities because
they *distrust* God's goodness and *disavow* God's cause. At the
heart of all natural religion is a deep suspicion and hostility
toward that last Power of life and death that moves through all
things. All natural religion is a flight from or a fight against
the "Terrible God" who calls all things into life and sends them
into death.[21] As such, natural faith is nothing other than radical
faith in a negative form, since radical faith calls men to trust
rather than to distrust, to serve rather than to combat that final
Power. Thus, the *overcoming* of natural faith and the *becoming*
of radical faith are two sides of a single and unending process
of being reconciled to God—of the Void and the Enemy becoming the Companion!

For Niebuhr, this reconciliation cannot be initiated by the
distrustful and disloyal creature.[22] Sinful man cannot transfer
his trust from gods to God or convert his loyalty from partial
causes to an inclusive cause. But Niebuhr points to an event in
history where God has taken the initiative to reconcile men to
himself and to all his creation. Recounting his own personal and
theological pilgrimage, he writes:

> How is it possible to rely on God as unconquerably loving and
> redeeming, to have confidence in him as purposive person work-
> ing toward the glorification of his creation and of himself in his
> works, to say to the great "IT," "Our Father who art in heaven"
> —this remains the miraculous gift. It is the human impossibility
> which has been made possible, as has also the enlistment of these

unlikely beings, these human animals, ourselves, in his cause, the cause of universal redemption. So far as I could see and can now see *that miracle has been wrought among us by and through Jesus Christ.*[23]

In the historical event of Jesus Christ, reconciliation to God and among men has been given and is available.

How then, according to Niebuhr, does Jesus Christ reconcile God and men? Since Niebuhr conceives of sin as false faith, salvation from sin means the transformation of natural faith into radical faith. Jesus Christ reconciles God and men by mediating radical faith.

THE MEDIATOR OF RADICAL FAITH

Niebuhr interprets the person and work of Jesus Christ in terms of his understanding of the triadic structure of faith. The self is always dynamically related, either negatively or positively, to God and to neighbor in the orders of being, valuing and knowing. This means that the quality and understanding of one's relationships to God and to neighbor are inseparably bound up with one another. The one cannot be renewed or altered without the other being recast or transformed. In other words, natural religion's flawed triad of idolatrous and partisan relationships can only be overturned by a concrete experience and historical demonstration of radical faith which embodies radical trust in God's absolute goodness and radical loyalty to God's universal cause. But such a disclosure lies beyond sinful selves. Only if sinful selves are taken into a relationship to God *and* neighbor which is uncompromised by suspicion and hostility will radical faith become intelligible and available to sinful selves. That, in turn, requires a neighbor who incarnates and mediates such radical faith. In Christian history and for Christian faith, that neighbor is none other than Jesus Christ.

Jesus Christ is the definitive Neighbor by and through whom radical faith is called forth in the Christian community. Niebuhr is aware of the danger of speaking of Jesus Christ as "neighbor" since some may erroneously take this to mean that Jesus Christ only reveals what it means to be human.[24] He *does* reveal that—a fact of faith repeatedly overlooked or obscured in the history of Christian thought—but Jesus Christ also reveals what it means to be divine. In Niebuhr's triadic scheme of faith, the axial moment of both disclosures is the radical faith of Jesus Christ. The movements of radical faith in loyalty toward the neighbor and in trust toward God are both impossible apart from the received assurance of the trustworthiness and loyalty of God. In other words, what it means to be truly God is given in and through what it means to be truly man. Thus, the radical faith of Jesus Christ mediates at once the human and the divine dimensions of radical faith.

In terms of classical christological formulae and discussion, Niebuhr interprets Jesus Christ as the union of two "wills" (the *prosopic* union of the human and the divine) rather than as the union of two "natures" [25] (the *hypostatic* union of the human and the divine). But unlike other christologies which stress the concrete humanity of Jesus, Niebuhr's christology is neither Pelagian nor Adoptionist. Niebuhr does not claim that Jesus *became* the supreme teacher and exemplar of the Christian life through personal resolve or moral obedience. To be sure, he assumes that Jesus was a real human being fulfilling a real human vocation in real human response to God. But, unlike the moralistic christologies of Pelagianism or Adoptionism, Niebuhr's account of Jesus' authentic relationship to God and neighbor is not modeled on an individualistic or a voluntaristic view of human nature and religious experience. Human life and faith are always and inescapably a reciprocal relationship between the self, neighbor and God *in which God is the prevenient member and mover*. Within this dynamic triad, Niebuhr's christology explicates the movement of Jesus toward God and every neighbor as faithful *response* to the movement of God toward Jesus and every neighbor. Within this structure of prevenience and response, he can then speak of Jesus Christ as the mediator of *both* true humanity and true divinity.

Jesus Christ mediates true humanity through his incarnation

of radical faith. Niebuhr typically uses the word "incarnation" to denote the concrete expression in human life of exclusive trust in God's goodness and universal loyalty to the whole realm of God's creation.[26] Radical faith, seemingly incarnate only in an ambiguous way in the life of the ancient Hebrews, appeared unambiguously in Jesus Christ. "The greatness of his confidence in the Lord of heaven and earth as fatherly goodness toward all creatures, the consistency of his loyalty to the realm of being, seem unqualified by distrust or by competing loyalty." Jesus accepted the assurance that God was wholly faithful to him and to all creatures, and he responded by being absolutely trustful of God and loyal to the whole of God's creation.[27]

Since faith permeates all practical and theoretical activity, Niebuhr finds the radical faith of Jesus Christ expressed in both word and deed.[28] Though Niebuhr has not dealt with the New Testament materials extensively, the manner in which he would use them to point to the "essence" in the "phenomena" of the faith of Jesus is indicated in several brief discussions of the life and death of Jesus Christ. For example, in *Christ and Culture*, Niebuhr singles out the "virtues" of love, hope, obedience, faith, and humility to manifest the double movement of Jesus Christ's radical confidence in God's goodness and radical loyalty to God's cause. This same confidence and loyalty is expressed even more clearly and resolutely in the death of Jesus Christ. Even death on the cross did not compromise his trust in God's faithfulness to him and to all creatures, or deflect his loyalty to every neighbor in being. Or again, in *The Responsible Self*, Niebuhr explores this manifestation of radical faith through examples of Jesus' interpretation and response to natural happenings, human relationships and personal suffering.[29] In other words, according to Niebuhr, the true humanity which Jesus mediates in and through his own radical faith is concretely embodied in word and deed, in thought and act, in life and death.

In light of his view of faith as a dynamic triad embracing self, neighbor and God, Niebuhr insists that a response to the faith *of* Jesus Christ involves more than faith *in* Jesus Christ.

Of course, in Niebuhr's scheme, Jesus Christ did and does com-
mand men's trust and loyalty by living as a trustworthy and
loyal man among men. But, as a man living among men, Jesus
Christ does not claim for himself the absolute trust and loyalty
that are due only to God. Niebuhr is well aware that popular
theology and personal piety often simply equate God and Jesus.
He calls this reduction of God to the one figure of Jesus Christ
"Christomonism." Yet, despite its persistence and power throughout Christian history, Niebuhr is convinced that it is theologically and practically pernicious—so pernicious in fact that he
speaks of such theology and piety as idolatrous! The ultimate
focusing of faith and worship in Jesus Christ seriously compromises God's sovereignty and recklessly aggrandizes the
church's faith.

Niebuhr is equally certain that his protest is no mere modern
innovation.[30] Christomonism is contrary to the overall biblical
witness, to trinitarian thought and to radical faith. *Biblically,*
the identification of God and Jesus is based on comparatively
few passages in the New Testament. More important, this selec-
tive exegesis contradicts biblical reports of Jesus' own testimony
about his vocation and relationship to God.[31] The biblical Jesus
points away from himself to God. Furthermore, Christomonism's
use of the Old Testament only insofar as it points to Jesus Christ
is a distortion of the Jewish faith and of the Christian scriptures.

Christomonism is also contrary to *trinitarian* thought.[32]
Though making use of different categories than did the Church
Fathers, Niebuhr affirms the importance of maintaining the
ontological and epistemological substance of trinitarian thought.
Ontologically, trinitarian thought recognizes that the God active
in Jesus Christ is the same God active in nature and present to
personal and social experience. Epistemologically, trinitarian
doctrine insists on the inseparability of the way God is known
in Jesus Christ and the way he is discovered in the creation and
in personal and social experience.

Christomonism's tendency toward a "unitarianism of the
second person of the Trinity" abridges both these concerns.
Ontologically, Christomonism tends to restrict God's action to

history or to personal experience, thereby overlooking the importance of being reconciled to the Lord of nature. As a consequence, creation and culture are typically regarded at best as the prologue and at worst as the antithesis of redemption. Thereby, Christomonism fails to illumine God's action in all of history and nature. It fails to deal with the more profound problems of human responsibility, suffering, and destiny. Epistemologically, Christomonism offers no cogent solution to the problem of how God is recognizable in Jesus Christ or recoverable in present experience other than the answers of biblical or revelational positivism.

Finally, Christomonism is contrary to *radical* faith.[33] Niebuhr is convinced that substituting the lordship of Christ for the lordship of God frequently issues in a self-defensive, self-glorifying henotheism. This is ironic, since the church seems so cognizant of the signs of particularism in Judaism. Despite this awareness, the church again and again absolutizes its own historical revelation and thus converts the God known in the Christian community to a Christian God. This transposition inevitably turns divine election from a call to service into a guarantee of status, redirects loyalty from every neighbor to the fellow churchman, rejects God's redemptive action in every event by confining that action to a "holy history."

To sum up, Niebuhr finds that all such simple identifications of God and Jesus Christ and all such restrictions of God's revelation and redemption exclusively to Jesus Christ fall dangerously short of biblical truth, trinitarian insight and radical faith. Instead, Niebuhr calls for a *confessional* theology that affirms God's redemptive and revelatory work in Jesus Christ without limiting that work to one historical event remembered by one historical community. Only such a confessional approach will guard the church against substituting Christian revelation, religion, or morality for God.[34]

Of course, Niebuhr's critique of Christomonism also draws support from the Chalcedonian Creed, which stipulates that the divine and the human "natures" are joined "without confusion, without change, without division, and without separation." But

the metaphysical language of Chalcedon does not clarify the
problem of the believer's relation to true human and true divinity in and through Jesus Christ. In contrast, by making a triadic
view of faith his central category for Christology, Niebuhr illumines how faith was and is related to *Jesus* while neither
equating Jesus with God nor directing ultimate trust to Jesus.
Within the Christian community, supreme *interhuman* trust and
loyalty are given to the definitive Neighbor Jesus, but *absolute*
trust and loyalty are reserved for God alone.

But here the great obstacle for radical faith comes to clear
focus. In the light of the shameful end of Jesus Christ, how can
men trust in the God in whom he trusted, be loyal to the cause
to which he was loyal? Does not the crucifixion of the trusting
and loyal Jesus Christ *confirm* rather than *dispel* man's distrust
of God's deity and disloyalty to God's cause? Facing this stone
of stumbling, Niebuhr declares "that unless there enters into our
existence the demonstration, as it were, of the loyalty of the
Lord of heaven and earth to this One who was so loyal to Him
and so loyal to his fellow man we can't believe God." [35] The
radical faith of Jesus Christ, whatever its exemplary heroism
and tragic beauty, is powerless to call forth radical faith in
others if death and meaninglessness have the final word over his
faith. Therefore, Niebuhr speaks of Jesus Christ as demonstrating and mediating the divine ground as well as the human side
of faith.

As suggested above, radical faith's relationship to God and
neighbor can never be abstracted from God's goodness and
faithfulness. But God's movement toward man does not *begin*
only when human resources fail or only when human efforts are
deserving. God, in Niebuhr's understanding, is no *deus ex
machina* or conditional benefactor. Rather, God's movement to
man is always preveniently present in man's movement to God.
Therefore, Jesus Christ's incarnation of radical faith, seen
whole, is a human *response* to divine *initiative*.[36]

But Niebuhr sees precisely this "paradox" of divine initiative and human response called into question by the crucifixion.[37]
If the radical faith of Jesus Christ has no trustworthy and loyal

Ground, then the cross stands as history's bitterest symbol of the final loss of all things given to man and of the final injustice of all burdens borne by him—the cross reveals unavoidable destruction and innocent suffering at the heart of things. At this razor's edge of despair, Niebuhr proclaims that a great surd enters. Supremely in the midst of this crisis, radical faith in the faithfulness and goodness of God is created:

> To some of us it seems that in the cross of Jesus Christ, in the death of such a man who trusts God and is responsible to him as a son, we face the great negative instance or the negation of the premise that God is love, and that unless this great negative instance—summarizing and symbolizing all the negative instances —is faced, faith in the universal power of God must rest on quicksand; in facing it, however, we have the demonstration in this very instance of a life-power that is not conquered, not destroyed. Reality maintains and makes powerful such life as this. The ultimate power does manifest itself as the Father of Jesus Christ through his resurrection from the dead. The resurrection is not manifest to us in physical signs but in his continuing Lordship— his session at the right hand of power, as the old creeds put it. So we apprehend the way God is manifested not in creation and destruction but in these *and* resurrection, in the raising of the temporal to the eternal plane.[38]

Thus the faith of Jesus and the faithfulness of God are focused in crucifixion and resurrection. The cross (where Jesus exemplifies radical faith even when God seems faithless) and the resurrection (where God sustains radical faith against the ravages of nothingness) belong together, but not as an "if-then" entailment or a "first this—then that" chronology. Rather they are inseparable aspects of the Christian community's historical revelation and contemporary paradigm of radical faith. In crucifixion and resurrection, human faith and divine faithfulness are one "without confusion, change, division or separation." [39]

This bond in radical faith between crucifixion as the paradigmatic demonstration of human faith and resurrection as the central disclosure of divine faithfulness raises the question of how and why they are connected. Is resurrection a divine reward for human fidelity beyond suffering and death, or is it the divine renewal of human faith amid suffering and death? To put it another way, does resurrection signal God's presence and power not merely over and beyond but also in and through suffering and death?

Niebuhr spells out no full answer to this problem, though he frequently deals with it in an elliptical fashion. In a variety of passages, Niebuhr makes it clear that God's judgment and redemption *are* wrought through suffering and death, even and especially through the suffering and death of the innocent. He further speaks of these sacrifices as somehow requiring God's sacrifice. In a typical passage, Niebuhr describes the cross as a "revelation, though 'in a glass darkly,' of the intense moral earnestness of a God who will not abandon mankind to self-destruction; it confronts us with the tragic consequences of moral failure. It does all this because it is sacrifice—the self-sacrifice of Jesus Christ for those whom he loves and God's sacrifice of his best-loved son for the sake of the just and the unjust." [40] Or again, in a more telling passage, Niebuhr writes, "Interpreted through the cross of Jesus Christ the suffering of the innocent is seen not as the suffering of temporal men but of the eternal victim 'slain from the foundations of the world.' "

Niebuhr's thoughts along these lines seem to imply that the crucifixion of Jesus Christ demonstrates that the perennial pain of *man* and the participating suffering of *God* are both inseparable elements in that reconstruction of faith and life expressed in the resurrection of Jesus Christ. But, though Niebuhr's images and arguments lead in this direction, he seems to stop short of claiming that God transmutes the creation's pain and loss by actually taking them into himself. He rests content with the assurance that God's resurrecting presence and power in all the events and relationships of life will deliver the faithful from suffering's absurdity and death's finality.

Niebuhr is no less tentative and teasing in his understanding of *how* the resurrection faith arose among the disciples. But, on the basis of his theological orientation in general and his occasional references to the rise of resurrection faith in particular, certain intimations of his thinking on the resurrection can be ventured.

First, regardless of how the resurrection "happened," it was the act of *God*.[41] Resurrection is not a human possibility, not even for essential or true humanity. It is solely the possibility of the Lord of life and death.

Second, regardless of how the resurrection "happened," it was apprehensible only by *faith*.[42] As an integral movement in the historical Gestalt of the revelatory event, the resurrection could not be experienced from a nonparticipating point of view. This means that the New Testament accounts of the resurrection are *faith* statements about an event in that faith's inner history, not historical reports of public occurrence.

Finally, regardless of how the resurrection "happened," it was the deliverance of *Jesus*. The rise of the resurrection faith is inexplicable apart from the radical faith of Jesus and the community of the faithful that gathered around him. The "Risen Christ" is the "same one whose deeds were described by those who 'from the beginning were eyewitnesses and ministers of the word.' "[43]

Obviously, these intimations are not an adequate statement of how Niebuhr does, in fact, account for the resurrection faith. They are sufficient, however, to indicate that he *rejects* all corporal literalizing and psychological subjectivizing of the resurrection "event." Since revelation is never given in external history, the resurrection of Jesus Christ must in some way be intimately connected with the elicitation of radical faith among the companions and followers of Jesus Christ in faith. But, unlike similar proposals among contemporary theologians such as John Knox and Rudolf Bultmann, Niebuhr's triadic and historic view of faith guards his approach from simply *equating* the resurrection of Jesus with the faith of the disciples. Jesus Christ *endures* in the Christian community as the center and symbol of man's reconciliation to God's universal goodness and cause. This is his reign as Risen Lord.[44]

How then is the radical faith of the Risen Lord appropriated

in the life of the contemporary Christian? We have seen that
Niebuhr rejects all supernatural and transhistorical connections
between the Christ event and his present-day followers. Jesus
Christ is no spiritual being supernaturally bestowing faith on
the believer. Nor is the radical faith of Jesus given through a
spiritual encounter with him born of biblical proclamation.
Rather, the radical faith of Jesus Christ is recognized and received as God's revelation and reconciliation in and through
its power to transform natural faith.

THE TRANSFORMATION OF RADICAL FAITH

Niebuhr's solution to the theological problem of the so-called
"point of contact" between revealing God and sinful man rests
on his understanding of natural faith as the perversion of radical faith.

> Man's good nature has become corrupted; it is not bad as
> something that ought not to exist, but warped, twisted and mis-
> directed. He loves with the love that is given him in his creation,
> but loves beings wrongly, in the wrong order; he desires good
> with the desire given him by his maker, but he aims at goods
> that are not good for him and misses his true good; he produces
> fruit, but it is misshapen and bitter; he organizes society with the
> aid of his practical reason, but works against the grain of things
> in self-willed forcing of his reason into irrational paths, and
> thus disorganizes things in his very act of organization.[45]

Natural man's relation to God and neighbor is neither essentially intact (liberalism) nor totally effaced (neoorthodoxy).
Thus Niebuhr's view that radical faith appears in a disordered
way as natural faith offers a "third way" between liberal and
neoorthodox interpretations of man's relationship to God apart
from historic revelation.

Accordingly, Niebuhr also offers a mediating view of the way
in which historic revelation is received and appropriated in the
lives of contemporary believers. The radical faith incarnate in
Jesus Christ comes neither as the historic *illustration* of a faith

essentially sound (liberalism) nor as a unique *demonstration* of a faith wholly absent (neoorthodoxy) but as the *transformation* of a faith thoroughly corrupted.[46] Under the impact of the radical faith of Jesus Christ, man's natural faith is continually revolutionized rather than historically confirmed or miraculously replaced.

Niebuhr describes this transformation by marking the revolution in both practical activity and theoretical understanding that comes with radical faith. Jesus Christ's disclosure of God's absolute trustworthiness and universal cause calls forth a new order of divine-human and interhuman relationships. Since these interpersonal relationships permeate all practical and theoretical activity, their transformation calls for the conversion of religious behavior and beliefs, of moral activity and standards. Moreover, though Niebuhr believes that practical relationships are logically prior to intellectual formulations in faith, relationships and beliefs are related dialectically. Hence in the experience of any given person, either one may come first chronologically. In concrete experience, some persons move from the transformation of their natural understanding of God and morality to a radical revolution in their personal relationships and conduct, while other persons move from the transformation of concrete trust-loyalty relationships to new interpretations of the nature and meaning of these changed relationships.

Niebuhr illustrates this transformation of natural faith in terms of the revolution in our common religious and moral understanding that revelation brings.[47] Revelation transforms all our natural ideas about divine unity, power and goodness. The God revealed in Jesus Christ has the integrity of a faithful person rather than the unity of a fixed order. The power of that God is not the power opposed to death but the power in and behind death that is stronger than death. The goodness of God made manifest in Jesus Christ is the creative goodness of forgiving love, not the exacting goodness of legal righteousness. In similar fashion Niebuhr describes the conversion of moral standards wrought by the revelatory event. The imperativeness of the moral law is shown to lie not in the demand of reason

or of society but in the God who continually disrupts and renews our rational understanding and social arrangements.
Revelation extends the moral law's intensiveness and extensive-
ness beyond the fellow believer and loved one to every neighbor
in being, whether friend or enemy, animate or inanimate, near
or far. Finally, revelation begins the permanent transformation
of the moral imperative into the moral indicative where love is
freely given without fear of punishment or hope of reward.

In this way, Niebuhr is able to show how revelation brings
new *relationships* and new *knowledge* without equating revelation with mystical encounter or propositional statements. At the
same time he answers the thorny theological problem of how
the revelation of God in Jesus Christ is recognized and appropriated by sinful man. God comes not as a personally and intellectually *unknown* God but as a personally and intellectually
unexpected God. He comes meeting all of man's expectations of
deity and duty, but transforms those expectations by disclosing
his absolute trustworthiness and his universal cause. He comes
reconciling distrustful and disloyal man to himself, putting an
end to strife among the finite gods and bringing wholeness to
personal and social existence.

But this transformation of relationships and concepts is not
confined to the Christian community, even though it is *discovered* within that community.

> The standpoint of the Christian community is limited, being
> in history, faith and sin. But what is seen from this standpoint
> is unlimited. Faith cannot get to God save through historic ex-
> perience as reason cannot get to nature save through sense experi-
> ence. But as reason, having learned through limited experience
> and intelligible patterns of reality, can seek the evidence of like
> patterns in all other experiences, so faith having apprehended the
> divine self in its own history can and must look for the manifesta-
> tion of the same self in other events.[48]

For the Christian community, Jesus Christ is its "Rosetta Stone"
for unlocking and interpreting all the strange signs and sounds
of its past, present and future as words of God.

THE EXTENSION OF RADICAL FAITH

Niebuhr notes that the attempt to relate God's action in Jesus Christ to God's action in all times and places has often presented a dilemma to theology.[49] In explicating Christ's significance for faith, the church has often chosen between the timeless truth and the unique fact of the Christ event. Jesus Christ is portrayed either as illustrating universal features of divine and human experience (in which case the Christ event seems historically accidental and dispensable), or as demonstrating unique expressions of divine and human action (in which case the Christ event is historically necessary and *sui generis*).

This dilemma does not arise in Niebuhr's analysis. Jesus Christ does reveal the constancy of divine behavior and the possibility of radical faith in all times and places. But, since God is present only to *historic* faith, Jesus Christ endures in the church as *its* normative disclosure of divine behavior and as *its* indispensable possibility of human response. Niebuhr compares this normative givenness and universal relevance to a decisive and unique moment in the common life of friends: "In the face of some emergency a man may act so as to reveal a quality undisclosed before. Through that revelatory moment his friend is enabled to understand past actions which had been obscure and to prophesy the future behavior of the revealer. But the revelatory moment not only disclosed constant features of conduct which had previously been hidden; it also introduced a new relation between the persons and remains a unique point in their history." [50] Thus Jesus Christ is at once irrevocably past and particular yet decisively present and relevant in Christian history and for Christian faith.

But how and why must contemporary Christians read the entire human past, present and future as the limitless work of God? How does the Christian community employ its mediator of radical faith to reason about the totality of human experience, and why is such an extension of radical faith to the whole sweep of history and nature vital to human wholeness?

The Christian community's revelation calls forth a faith which is relevant to the whole range of reason's activity. For Niebuhr, reason criticizes and compares, refines and relates the whole of sensory and believing experience. Reason's practical task of interpreting internal history is always dependent upon some concrete standpoint in history and faith. For the Christian, the event of Jesus Christ furnishes the constructs and companions, the images and interpreters through which the confusions of personal existence and the brawl of communal histories can be woven together into a "theology" of history in which God is active in every event (past, present and future).[51] Furthermore, Niebuhr contends that radical faith can even make a contribution to theoretical reasoning about external history. Although the revelation in Jesus Christ does not furnish information about the external world, radical faith can furnish a context of "disinterested" and objective truth-seeking and truth-telling which frees theoretical reasoning from the necessity of defending and guarding the interests of selves and communities.[52] Thus Niebuhr believes that Jesus Christ disclosed and mediates a radical faith which equips practical reason with the patterns and companions necessary for making a whole of past, present and future experiences of devotion and duty. Radical faith also liberates pure reason to pursue knowledge of all natural, biological, psychological, and sociological phenomena without fear of undermining the self's vital values and causes.

All this reasoning on the basis of revelation is directed toward the achievement of personal and social wholeness.[53] The evil imaginations of natural faith divide men within themselves and separate them from one another.[54] But, with the adequate symbols or metaphors derived from the revelatory event, the Christian community can find concilatory patterns and meanings in all of human life and history. Tracing in all events the working of one God, it can apprehend in the entire human past God's provision, in the entire human present God's purpose, in the entire human future God's possibility.[55] Far from being a mere intellectual exercise, such interpretive reconstruction is a vital part of any integration of the self and of any community with the neighbor. There can be no personal integrity or human community without *unified* memories, concerns and hopes. Ultimately, the whole sweep of human history and natural process must be viewed as a single epic. The entire universe—animate and inanimate, natural and historical, individual and collective —must be entered into as the one family of the Father God, as the one kingdom of the Sovereign God. The Christian finds the only enduring core of individual selfhood and universal community in the one God who is active in *every* event as he was active in the Christ Event.

Finally then, Jesus Christ does not accomplish salvation apart from man's participation. Such participation involves *living by faith* in a new order of personal relationships and *reasoning in faith* about the whole context and range of human experience. But, in this personal dialectic of faithful life and thought, Jesus Christ remains faith's commission and possibility. As Niebuhr puts it: "We climb the mountain of revelation that we may gain a view of the shadowed valley in which we dwell and from the valley we look up again to the mountain. Each arduous journey brings new understanding, but also new wonder and surprise. This mountain is not one we climbed once upon a time; it is a well-known peak we never wholly know, which must be climbed again in every generation, on every new day." [56] The Christian community must continually go beyond but always return to its particular revelation in its particular history as it lives by faith in the world.

CONCLUSION: THE REVELATION-FAITH COMPLEX

In conclusion, when Niebuhr's formal analysis of external and internal history is joined with his concrete discussions of natural and radical faith, the content and standpoint of his theology of revelation stand clear.

Ontologically, the distinction between external and internal history establishes revelation as simultaneously ordinary occurrence and religious event. But the concrete manner of this duality in union rests on faith's triadic structure of divine-human relationships embodied in all cognitive and conative activity. Therefore Niebuhr locates faith's interrelation between self, God and others in the historic phenomena (both words and deeds) in which this interrelation is embodied.

Epistemologically, external and internal history mark distinctive standpoints for discerning history's duality in union. But these differing aspects are always concretely apprehended through historic categories and alongside historic companions. Radical faith's categories and companions are present in a community created and sustained by the living memory of a revelatory event. Thus Niebuhr bases radical faith's apprehension of God, others, and self, in the historic community (both past and present) through which this interrelation is understood.

Soteriologically, the distinction between external and internal history explains why revelation in history may be affirmed or denied. History is apprehended as revelatory only under and with the categories and companions of radical faith. But this cognitive and social standpoint is not a universal structure of possibility for human beings. Thus Niebuhr grounds radical faith's reconciliation between self, others and God in the historic event of Jesus Christ (both *extra nos* and *pro me*) by which this interrelation is established.

Seen in these terms, perhaps a more appropriate geometric model than a simple triad can be found for visualizing and summarizing the complete structure and substance of Niebuhr's theology of revelation.[57] For Niebuhr, God is never known apart from his relation to the self and the neighbor. Within the Christian community, Jesus Christ is the great Neighbor who initiates a new order of interpersonal relationships and calls forth a new interpretation of reality. But since Jesus Christ is an event in the past he cannot be known apart from the mediation of a remembering community. For this reason, a *triangle* (God, Jesus Christ, self) does not convey the full complexity of Niebuhr's view of revelation and faith, since the self's relation to Jesus Christ is not transhistorical. Niebuhr's revelation-faith complex is more adequately modeled by a *tetrahedron* whose apex is God and whose triangular base is formed by self, neighbor and Jesus Christ. The *base* of the tetrahedron (self, neighbor, Jesus Christ) represents the historic community which mediates the normative disclosure of faith to the contemporary community which is the *face* of the tetrahedron (self-neighbor-God).

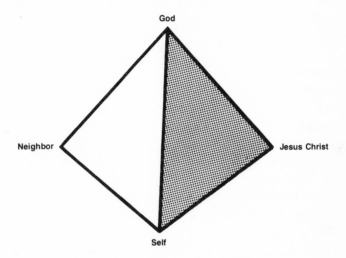

Jesus Christ transmitted through the neighbor in the church is the enduring and normative great Neighbor with whom the self responds to God and neighbor and through whom God acts on the self and neighbor.

Part Three

NIEBUHR
AS
ETHICIST

VII. A Theory of Responsibility

THE CONTEXT OF MORAL BEHAVIOR

For H. Richard Niebuhr ethics is a reflective examination of the moral life in search of self-knowledge and practical guidance.[1] Like all reflective efforts, ethics does not create the phenomenon it investigates. It hopes, however, to modify that subject matter by clarifying or changing the morality people already have. But Neibuhr's conception of how ethical reflection contributes to moral integrity and transformation differs from most theological and philosophical accounts of the moral life. He does not furnish a manual of specific moral rules or goals governing typical situations. Nor does he prescribe a formal law or ideal which determines every conceivable moral decision. He sees the task of the moral theologian or the moral philosopher preceding such regulative principles and situational applications. His task is to explore *ethos*—to lay bare the underlying sentiments and fundamental character of a community's moral life. Only when moral awareness is thus fully informed can moral decisions be properly formed. Niebuhr's work as an ethicist aims at comprehending this full context of moral behavior rather than enunciating the specific guidelines of moral decision.

This unwillingness to prescribe laws to be obeyed or ideals to be pursued follows directly from Niebuhr's overall conception of the moral life. He belongs to a small but growing group of religious and secular ethicists who analyze morality in terms of *responsibility*.[2] For these thinkers the concept of responsibility furnishes a new and promising way for interpreting moral behavior and its supporting context. This concept suggests that morality is more a matter of relationships than of principles, of situations than of obligations, of dialogue than of calculation. More particularly, for Niebuhr "responsibility" gathers together the moral life in a way strikingly similar to the way that "faith" articulates the religious life. These turn out on inspection to be distinctive but parallel ways to talk about the one interactional field that embraces self, God and neighbor.

Niebuhr does not delimit the use of responsibility to the interpretation of Christian ethics. He believes that this new central notion proves equally insightful and incisive for analyzing all styles of morality and systems of ethics.[3] This general applicability of the idea of responsibility proves quite useful for Niebuhr's work as a Christian ethicist. It establishes a "universe of discourse" for comparing and contrasting, for criticizing and assimilating other styles and systems of morality to his own.

Not that Niebuhr is bent on claiming the superiority or finality of Christian ethics. As we shall see presently, he is just as critical of defensiveness or exclusivism in Christian ethics as in Christian theology. But Niebuhr's "confessional" approach whether in ethics or in theology does not exclude critical rejections and constructive syntheses of other accounts. His fondness for finding a mediating way between polar opposites which avoids their weaknesses and consolidates their strengths is just as evident in his ethical as in his theological work. In both, Niebuhr characteristically searches not so much for a new position as for a new combination—a bringing together through mediation and transformation of what has formerly been apart and at odds. Indeed, this is the process of perpetual repentance and reformation that Niebuhr sees as the heart of Christian faith and the bedrock of reality.

Accordingly in Part Three we will first examine Niebuhr's

phenomenology of responsibility—his general theory of the elemental components and the intentional constants of responsible action regardless of the particular context and content of that action. Then we will explore the distinctive content and context of moral responsibility in radical monotheism as seen in the lives of selves and communities.

THE METAPHOR OF RESPONSIBILITY

As we saw in the third chapter, Niebuhr's search for a viable ethics led him to an entirely new conception of the moral life. That search taught him that more was required than simply refining the rules or refurbishing the ideals of Christian ethics. His personal and theological recovery of the centrality of God and the pervasiveness of faith in all human experience demanded a complete recasting of the moral life. He saw that morality must somehow be understood as an inescapable relation to God and as a dynamic dimension of faith. Niebuhr found such a new mold for Christian ethics in the idea of "responsibility." He made brief use of this term as early as *The Social Sources of Denominationalism* in a discussion of the irresponsibility of the divided church.[4] But over the succeeding years he pioneered a full theory of moral responsibility which explicates the root metaphor, analyzes the essential elements and characterizes the dominant forms of responsibility.

Niebuhr commends responsibility as a newly emerging account of the moral life. As such, responsibility rivals or replaces two other long-employed descriptions of human conduct and moral decision.[5] *Teleological* theories of ethics interpret the moral life in terms of the goals of human behavior and the consequences of human choice. What these goals are and how these consequences are weighed are matters of disagreement among teleologists. But all agree that morality is fundamentally a matter of the purposive shaping of life toward future and final goals. *Deontological* theories of ethics, by contrast, understand morality as a matter of timeless rules and strict compliance. Deontologists also differ among themselves over the source and the sum of the regulations that govern human conduct and relationships. But they all assume without argument that morality is principled obedience or legal conformity to some reign of law.

Niebuhr willingly admits that these comprehensive accounts have had a long and helpful history of explaining and guiding moral behavior. But in advocating a new account of morality as responsibility, Niebuhr catalogs a number of deficiencies and difficulties with the more venerable teleological and deontological theories.[6] Each lacks comprehensiveness and consistency. In practical application, the two conflicting theories seem to require each other to make sense out of moral choice and change. Quandaries over rights and obligations in real life oscillate between debates over ideals to be pursued and laws to be obeyed —which laws embody the ideals that ought to shape individual and social existence? Which goals are consonant with the laws of human nature or divine righteousness? Niebuhr suggests that these deficiencies reveal that teleological and deontological theories are too remote from moral practice to illumine moral conduct adequately.

Niebuhr traces these failings to the *images* underlying the theories. As we saw in the first chapter, "root metaphors" or "symbolic forms" play a crucial role in thinking.[7] All reflection, whether about facts or values, proceeds by elaborating certain images or models, metaphors or symbols into intelligible constructs and meaningful connections within experience. In searching out the limitations of the teleological and deontological theories of ethics, Niebuhr reverses the process—he moves from elaborated theory back to root metaphor. The root metaphor of teleological theories of right and wrong is the common experience of craftsmanship. Modeled on this analogy, moral man fashions himself and his society much as he constructs tools and toys. Morality is the artful actualizing of certain goals. The means if not the ends are under human control and admit to differences in execution and achievement. By contrast, the root metaphor underlying deontological ethics is the equally familiar experience of citizenship.[8] The political image of making and obeying laws places a very different reading on moral experience than the one offered by the craftsman image. Here the moral life is regimented into entirely predictable and uniform behavior. Neither the means nor the ends of moral existence are situationally contingent.

Niebuhr's laying bare the fundamental images that inspire and inform teleological and deontological theories of ethics helps him pinpoint their shortcomings. Each theory illumines only a part of the total context and content of moral behavior. "Man-the-maker" theories of ethics help make sense of human freedom and historical change in moral action, but they underestimate the facticities of life and the importance of the human past. They do not fully perceive how life stubbornly resists human design, nor do they understand the impact of the past on present and future experience. As a consequence, teleological theories do not adequately account for the place of guilt, tragedy and character in the moral life. "Man-the-citizen" ethics clarify the importance of objectivity and impartiality in moral judgment and offer a clear rationale for moral instruction and discipline. But they reflect even less awareness of the temporality and solidarity of moral existence than do teleological accounts. They show little appreciation for life's ambiguity and history's novelty. Consequently, deontological theories offer little illumination of anxiety, freedom and change in the moral life. Niebuhr concludes that these great rival images of moral man, though helpful and instructive in their own right, are only very rough and approximate copies of the lived experience they reflect.[9] Something more and something different is required to bring the whole of morality into clearer focus.

Niebuhr finds such an alternative in the image of responsibility. What is implicit in the idea of responsibility is the image of "man-the-answerer"—man engaged in dialogue, man responding to action upon him.[10] For those who are trying to understand the whole of morality in light of this image, Niebuhr declares:

Now we think of all our actions as having the pattern of what we do when we answer another who addresses us. To be engaged in

dialogue, to answer questions addressed to us, to defend ourselves
against attacks, to reply to injunctions, to meet challenges—this
is a common experience. And now we try to think of all our actions as having this character of being responses, answers, to
actions upon us.[11]

Niebuhr believes that this "synecdochic analogy" corresponds
more fully to moral experience than either the maker or the
citizen analogies because it establishes a more inclusive and
personal context for moral reflection. Unlike the older images
and their variously elaborated theories, the dialogical metaphor
is fully consonant with the latest interactional theories of human
life in such disciplines as biology, psychology, sociology and
history. More important, it makes sense of moral action in social emergencies and personal suffering—those "limit experiences" in which the fundamental character of morality is
revealed precisely because it is threatened.[12] In such crises,
moral action is more a matter of situational response to challenges than of pursuing ideals or adhering to laws, since crisis
experiences fall outside of envisioned purposes or assumed
order.

Finally, Niebuhr notes that responsibility not only has great
affinities with modern thought and situations *in extremis* but
it also comports more nearly to the biblical ethos.[13] Efforts to
interpret the morality of ancient Israel or early Christianity
in terms of idealism and eschatology or of obedience and legal-
ism have always done violence to the scriptures. Both the Old
and New Testaments, considered whole, see morality as situational responses to what God is doing and requiring in concrete
situations. Thus Niebuhr looks for new clarity and comprehensiveness to come from ethical theories that rest on the image of
man-the-answerer.

In typical restraint when arguing for his own position, Niebuhr eschews having found in responsibility *the* key to understanding the Christian ethos.[14] He acknowledges a continuing
importance for teleological and deontological thinking even in
Christian ethics. But Niebuhr's comparative analysis of these

three positions clearly argues for responsibility's superior adequacy if not its ability to creatively combine its rivals. Thus, in a summary comparison, Niebuhr can observe:

> If we use value terms then the differences among the three approaches may be indicated by the terms, the *good,* the *right* and the *fitting;* for teleology is concerned always with the highest good to which it subordinates the right; consistent deontology is concerned with the right, no matter what may happen to our goods; but for the ethics of responsibility the *fitting* action, the one that fits into a total interaction as response and as anticipation of further response, is alone conducive to the good and alone is right.[15]

In short, responsibility's proximity to moral experience and its powers of synthesis are sufficient to convince Niebuhr that morality *should* be interpreted and guided in this way.

The systematic development of the metaphor of man-the-answerer has not proceeded far among those making use of it. Niebuhr's book *The Responsible Self* is at best a kind of prolegomena to a systematic ethics modeled on responsibility. But if this book is combined with stenographic transcriptions of his ethics lectures and other selected publications, Niebuhr does furnish an extended sketch of the basic elements and forms of responsibility as a general theory of the moral life.

THE ELEMENTS OF RESPONSIBILITY

Niebuhr is aware that metaphors in themselves do not interpret or guide experience. Symbols are laden with meaning and feeling, but these treasures must be mined by the intellect. A metaphor's hidden references, allusions and similes must be brought to the surface in order to serve human thought and moral life. So with the image of "man-the-answerer." If responsibility is to be useful for moral theory and practice, it must be given some precise meaning. Only then can its possibilities and limitations as an instrument of ethical understanding and guidance be explored and assessed.

As noted in the third chapter, Niebuhr's earliest elaboration
on the meaning of responsibility turns on the distinction between
"responsibility to" and "responsibility for." [16] There he argues
that moral responsibility is a universal feature of the social
life of men and as such always involves a double movement.

> To be responsible is to be able and required to give account
> *to* someone *for* something. The idea of responsibility, with the
> freedom and obligation it implies, has its place in the context
> of social relations. To be responsible is to be a self in the presence
> of other selves, to whom one is bound and to whom one is able
> to answer freely; responsibility includes stewardship or trustee-
> ship over things that belong to the common life of the selves.
> The question about the one *to* whom account must be rendered is
> of equal importance with the question about the what *for* which
> one must answer. [17]

Seen from this view, moralities differ over the "to-whom" and
the "for-what" of responsibility. If we must make answer only
to the nation or the denomination or the family, then we are
accountable only for those companions who answer to the same
claim that we do. By contrast, if we respond to a universal
God, then the neighbors for whom we are responsible include
the total society over which God presides. In short, the content
and scope of responsibility varies with the central nature of the
society to which we belong.

In *The Responsible Self*, Niebuhr elaborates this double
movement of responsibility into a general theory of responsibility with four essential elements.

> The idea or pattern of responsibility, then, may summarily and
> abstractly be defined as the idea of an agent's action as response
> to an action upon him in accordance with his interpretation of
> the latter action and with his expectation of response to his re-
> sponse; and all of this in a continuing community of agents. [18]

In other words, the four components in Niebuhr's delineation
of responsibility are response, interpretation, accountability
and social solidarity.

Responsiveness is both the precondition and realization of moral discernment and decision. Only when men respond do they take responsibility and become responsible. Responsiveness is a crucial category for Niebuhr's ethical analysis because it underlines the social and emotional dimensions of moral action. Beyond the obvious fact that moral action always occurs in a social setting, Niebuhr contends that the very capacity for moral discernment and judgment is actualized in response to ambient others. Drawing on the "dialogical" thinking of such men as George H. Mead, Josiah Royce and Martin Buber, he sees conscience and freedom, character and discipline as products as well as expressions of social responsiveness.[19]

Niebuhr further claims that moral responsiveness is emotionally evoked and energized as well as socially formed and directed. As we saw earlier, encounters with persons and values are mediated through emotional data—the "affections of the self." Personal and moral discernment are not logical inferences drawn from sensory impressions. Rather they are imaginative orderings of human feelings such as love and hate, sorrow and joy, fear and hope. Like Jonathan Edwards before him, Niebuhr conceives of moral action as the elemental responsiveness of the human heart to actions and claims upon us. In short, the primary element in all moral action is social and affective responsiveness.

Despite the importance of the affections in moral affairs, responsibility is not a merely emotive or intuitive response to the society that acts upon men. Human reaction is moral action only if it is a response to *interpreted* action.[20] Niebuhr insists that "the heart must reason; the participating self cannot escape the necessity of looking for pattern and meaning in its life and relations." [21] Interpretation is required because moral response, as distinguished from human reflex, always involves judgment and decision. Feelings can move the will, but only understanding can guide the will. Moral response must be informed by "an intelligence which identifies, compares, analyzes and relates events so that they come to us not as brute actions, but as understood and as having meaning." The patterns thus derived shape and sanction moral response. Such interpretation is imaginatively and historically funded. Moral reasoning is not so much deliberately applying moral principles to situations as interpreting situations in the light of events and experiences from the past which have decisively shaped personal and communal life. These events and experiences are distilled into impressions and images which the reasoning heart employs to fashion moral understanding and guidance.[22] Morality, then, requires responsive action in accordance with an interpretation of what is going on and of what is fitting. As Niebuhr bluntly puts it: "We respond as we interpret the meaning of action upon us." [23]

The third element is *accountability*.[24] Niebuhr points out that responsibility requires moral agents to be accountable for their responses—to stand behind them, to stay with them. Accountability is closely bound up with interpretation, since taking account of personal actions can only be done if they are placed in a time-frame of past circumstances and future consequences.

> Our actions are responsible not only insofar as they are reactions to interpreted actions upon us but also insofar as they are made in anticipation of answers to our answers. An agent's action is like a statement in a dialogue. Such a statement not only seeks to meet, as it were, or to fit into, the previous statement to which it is an answer, but is made in anticipation of reply. It looks forward as well as backward; it anticipates objections, confirmations and corrections. It is made as part of a total conversation that leads forward and is to have meaning as a whole.[25]

Thus, being accountable means exhibiting that dependability which insures the continuity and consistency of every moral action.

This call for accountability brings into view Niebuhr's fourth and final component of responsibility, *social solidarity*.[26] In stressing social solidarity, Niebuhr has more in mind than the fact that moral actions take place within a social setting and that moral consciousness arises within a social setting. Rather, responsibility is impossible unless all members of a community of moral agents maintain a relatively consistent scheme of interpretations of what is going on. Only such a shared and stable scheme of interpretation makes communal harmony and personal integrity possible in the face of the varied circumstances calling forth response. "Our action is responsible, it appears, when it is response to action upon us in a continuing discourse or interaction among beings forming a continuing society." Responsible action takes place only in a community of interpretation and accountability bound together in common cause and reciprocal loyalty.

Speaking of moral responsibility in terms of causes and loyalties calls to mind Niebuhr's analysis of faith. This association is by no means gratuitous. Niebuhr's interpretation of faith as that structure of trust-loyalty relationships which determines life's worth and duty directly parallels his analysis of morality in terms of responsiveness and responsibility.[27] Every moral community and ethical system pivots on a "center of value" which ultimately determines individual worth and duty. Such moral centers of value are equivalent to the God or gods of faith since they are affirmed in trust and served in loyalty.[28] For Niebuhr, all moral existence and responsive action are structured and sanctioned by some form of faith.

THE FORMS OF RESPONSIBILITY

In the strictest sense, the forms of responsibility are as diverse as the varieties of faith which support and sustain them. Of course, Niebuhr has simplified the multiplicity of faiths with his threefold distinction between polytheism, henotheism and radical monotheism. He makes occasional use of these categories to distinguish different forms of response ethics.[29] More typically, he employs the even simpler division between natural faith and radical faith to classify the general forms of responsibility. Finally all moralities divide over their underlying and implicit response to the ultimate context within which all things and persons, activities and relationships have their being and value. As we have seen, natural faith responds to that final context in suspicion and hostility while radical faith responds in trust and loyalty. These two kinds of faith have their moral counterparts in defensive and faithful forms of responsibility.[30]

Defensiveness: The Response of Natural Faith

Niebuhr maintains that defensiveness lies behind most human response. Such protectiveness is certainly due in part to the social nature and unfinished character of human existence. Human beings are social creatures who depend on others for their sustenance and self-esteem, and they are aspiring creatures who continually reach for new levels of experience and achievement. Because all such social interaction and self-making are laden with guilt and anxiety, we are prone to react defensively by way of protecting ourselves and our positions, our projects and actions. But Niebuhr traces this "fight or flight" responsiveness to deeper causes and conditions than human sociality and temporality. Finally, defensiveness reflects and projects a deep mistrust and antagonism toward life's ultimate context and final meaning. The morality of natural man is always a defense against meaninglessness which, from the standpoint of Christian faith, is a protest against God.

Niebuhr derives and defends this reading of man's characteristic moral defensiveness in two ways—philosophically and theologically. First, setting aside his own Christian commitments for purposes of philosophical analysis, Niebuhr explains how defensiveness arises out of the communal and contingent character of all moral life. Moral man exists socially in a vast number of communities, many with a distinctive ethos. Under such conditions, responsibilities are bound to clash and adjudications are unavoidable. Out of these typical conflicts and compromises, moral man is driven toward an encompassing community which will unify his responses and integrate his responsibilities. The demands of social life seem to require him to interpret and react to events *as if* they obeyed one pattern, formed one whole. But each claim to draw the boundaries of that whole, to master the design of that pattern, encounters competitors and detractors. The search for a universal community *within* space and time, human life and natural order, remains embattled, no matter how wide the circle is drawn—even humanism confronts an alien environment and naturalism an unavoidable entropy, to say nothing of less comprehensive moralities.

Such successless drives toward universality, Niebuhr explains, betray the radical contingency of all things human and natural. "The self that knows itself in encounter with others, finds itself to be absolutely dependent in its existence, completely contingent, inexplicably present in its here-ness and now-ness." Or again, "the radical action by which I am I and by which I am present with this body, this mind, this emotional equipment, this religion, is not identifiable with any of the finite actions that constitute the particular elements in physical, mental, personal existence." Though religion and culture are ways of screening out this sense of sheer dependence, Niebuhr believes that it is never fully contained or concealed from human view. Each failed quest for an encompassing community to unify existence and center responsibility portends a panic and a terror that cannot be borne. It quickens the self's secret fear "that though it is living, it is powerless to live; that though it may die, it is powerless to die; and that altogether, at every instant and in every particular, it is in the hands of some alien and inscrutable power."[31] Each such failure redoubles the resolve to defend those finite loves and loyalties that "help us make it through the night."

Niebuhr also interprets this descent into defensiveness from a theological perspective. From the standpoint of radical faith, all the moralities of natural man are defenses against God.[32] Both the human longing for a universal community and the human sense of sheer contingency are "signals of transcendence"—expressions at once of man's capacity and hunger for God. Yet natural religion and natural morality remain captive to dark suspicion and deep dread of life's ultimate context and meaning. Is the mysterious power that throws us into existence God? Then where is his goodness in a world that ends in destruction? Is the precious goodness that maintains us in existence God? Then where is his power in a world where goodness does not reign? Read from the vantage point of a radically mono-theistic faith, human morality grows out of distrust and dis-loyalty toward the radical action of God since God is perceived as consuming Void and implacable Enemy. Indeed, Niebuhr declares, "there is no atheistic morality; it is either theistic or anti-theistic." [33]

Drawing on this combined philosophical and theological analysis of defensiveness, Niebuhr sees natural morality as a "wisdom of survival." All such responses are devoted to con-structing and applying schemes for securing life's goods and services and for outliving friends and foes. Niebuhr labels these schemes of self-defensiveness the "ethics of death." [34] The personal expression of the ethics of death is self-preserva-tion, while its social counterpart is the closed society. Either or both may be narrowly self-serving, as egoistic and totalitarian moralities plainly demonstrate, but they need not be so. Stoi-cism's noble resignation and humanism's inclusive generosity are examples of natural moralities touched with unselfishness and compassion. But all natural moralities are bent on staving off the death of meaning and the death of belonging. And they thereby remain defensive against all things and all others who fall outside their circle of loves and loyalties. The ethics of death, like the gods of natural religion, are in the end divisive of life and defenseless against death.

Against this grim picture of human morality generally, Nie-buhr marks out another form of responsibility. To be sure, this form is in our history and our midst "more as hope than as datum, more perhaps as a possibility than as an actuality." [35] But a faithfulness has been given and is being given which transforms the ethics of death into the ethics of life—replacing self-preservation with self-giving, refashioning the closed society into the open society.[36] While the meaning of that faithfulness will be fully analyzed in the next two chapters, something of its general shape must be sketched here to round out Niebuhr's general phenomenology of responsibility.

Faithfulness: The Response of Radical Faith

For Niebuhr confidence in the goodness and trustworthiness of existence is not natural to man, but it is necessary for sustained moral action. Natural morality's anxious drive for individual integrity and universal community can find no surcease short of responding to one ultimate action in all interaction occurring within one inclusive society embracing all associations. But the assurance that we respond to one action upon us within one community that includes us is not enough in itself to sustain moral action. Natural moralities are haunted by just such a conviction—that we respond to one reality within one community—yet they are perceived as death-dealing rather than life-giving. Because of this suspicion and fear, natural moralities settle for some lesser power and narrower community to dignify life and define duty. Apparently human beings need a center and circle of *positive* value more than internal consistency and global unity. But, Niebuhr maintains, a fully effective morality requires both—a sense of individual worth and consistent responsiveness, a sense of social value and universal harmony. Only a morality grounded in one steadfast Other whose love and loyalty to *all* creatures never wavers can free men from the necessity of establishing their own worth. Only a morality exercised in one beloved Community embracing *all* creatures can free men from the necessity of favoring their own. In short, Niebuhr sees every morality sooner or later dissolving into divisiveness and defensiveness if it does not rest on a structure of radical faithfulness wherein all creatures are bound together by loyalty and trust in the trustworthy and loyal God.

This is not to say that men cannot live admirable lives without a belief in God. Niebuhr acknowledges and appreciates those who live decently and even heroically apart from any assurance that the universe is meaningful and friendly. Nor is it to deny that men seldom think about the universal setting and significance of their acts. Our daily rounds call for hundreds of responses that can and must be made quite apart from detailed analysis and comprehensive schemes. But Niebuhr is convinced that even trivial decisions and routine actions reveal an underlying attitude about whether the cosmos is indifferent (Void), inimical (Enemy) or hospitable (Companion). He further contends that men will not pursue their hopes and invest their energies without some sense of receptivity and endurance to their efforts. Human activity requires *some* reliable center and context for life's worth. But the "logic of death" at work in natural faith and natural morality compels Niebuhr to conclude that nothing short of "the Lord of life and death" can fulfill that need.

Where then can such faithfulness be found? How can it be achieved? From our discussion of sin and salvation in the last section, we can assume that natural morality does not represent the complete absence of radical faith but rather its total corruption. Natural moralities like natural religions are expressions of radical faith in *negative* form. Radical faith is the underlying datum and ever-present possibility for natural morality. This is what Niebuhr has in mind when he speaks of "the seed" of individual integrity and universal community that haunts natural morality. This is what he assumes when he puzzles over the process of *coming* to radical faith: "It remains questionable whether the self is led more to trust in the ultimate because it finds all the finite beings about it unreliable, or more because it is led by stages from trust in the near-at-hand to trust in the ultimate. Is it because all finite powers on which we have relied for value have failed us that we turn to the ultimate? Or, because we have seen traces of the structure of faith in the whole realm of being that we are led to confidence in Being simply considered?" [37]

This same metaphysical conviction underlies his guarded acknowledgments that radical faith is not limited to the community that remembers Jesus Christ:

> We do not fail to note that among our companions who refuse to take the name of Christian responses to action are made that

seem to be informed by the trust, the love of all being, the hope in the open future, that have become possible to us only in our life with Jesus Christ and in the presence of the One whom he encountered in all his encounters and to whom he gave fitting answer in all his answers to his companions. We believe that [this] reinterpretation of existence has come into the world and that it is not confined to those who say, "Lord, Lord," nor even necessarily best represented by them.[38]

For Niebuhr, radical faith is *always* present in *any* event of *every* life, albeit in twisted and perverted forms, else how *could* God be sovereign and good!

Nevertheless, whenever and wherever radical faith appears in positive form, it comes as both a revelation and a reconciliation. As such, it does not come without personal response and participation. It is not given apart from the wrestling with despair, the insight of imagination, the struggle of reason, and the discipline of will.[39] But something more than personal experience and effort is required—a demonstration of human faithfulness and divine trustworthiness in our communal and personal histories. For the Christian (and Niebuhr believes Christians may speak only for themselves), the event of Jesus Christ is where this revelation of faithfulness has been given and this reconciliation in faithfulness has begun:

> The responsible self we see in Christ and which we believe is being elicited in all our race is a universally and eternally responsive I, answering in universal society and in time without end, in all actions upon it, to the action of the One who heals all our diseases, forgives all our iniquities, saves our lives from destruction, and crowns us with everlasting mercy.[40]

Jesus Christ incarnates "infinite responsibility in an infinite universe," and he mediates that same faithfulness to all who receive him as the paradigm of the responsible life.[41]

Niebuhr, then, offers a general theory of responsibility for interpreting all moral action and reinterpreting all ethical systems. Rather than regarding morality as a matter of desired ends (teleology) or absolute norms (deontology), he proposes that we understand morality in terms of fitting responses (responsibility). Thus construed, every moral act is a socially informed and affectively charged response to action upon us, guided by some interpretive scheme of worth and accountability which the individual respondent shares in common with a continuing community of responsibility. At work in all such responses is some fundamental attitude and understanding of life's entire scheme of things. These fundamental orientations finally reduce to only two possible forms of response—defensiveness or faithfulness toward the universal context of moral action. But, though faithfulness seems demanded by the inherent dynamics of responsibility, it is present in natural moralities only as possibility and need. Thus natural morality points beyond itself to the ethics of radical monotheism. We must now see how Niebuhr's account of the particular content and context of moral responsibility in radical monotheism follows from this general theory of responsibility.

VIII. The Responsible Self

Niebuhr finds in the concept of responsibility an ideal framework for explicating the ethics of radical monotheism. This affinity is due in large measure to the fact that Niebuhr develops his theory of responsibility "from scratch" rather than taking over or modifying someone else's analysis of responsibility. Indeed, Niebuhr has done more than anyone else to develop this notion thematically among those who are exploring this mode of ethical reflection. Doubtless, Niebuhr's general theory of responsibility has been shaped in more than subtle ways by the particular moral tradition that he ultimately intends to illuminate. But, even setting aside the conscious and unconscious influences of Niebuhr's Christian faith, the image and the idea of responsibility are quite amenable to his purposes. Responsibility is a useful category for bringing together the key features of his analysis of radical faith—God's singular sovereignty and personal prevenience with man's communal nature and continual renewal. Responsibility furnishes Niebuhr an interactional framework for an ethics which does not separate religion and morality or the individual and society.

How Niebuhr interweaves these themes can best be seen by analyzing his approach to personal and communal morality.

Such a distinction should not be confused with the common practice in some theological circles of separating personal and social ethics. Niebuhr has no sympathy with such separation—as if the responsibilities of friendship and intimacy are somehow fundamentally different from those of citizenship and legality. But he does distinguish between the morality of individuals and of institutions, between the responsible self and the responsible church.

As an ethicist, Niebuhr directs most of his attention to the study and understanding of the responsible self. There is, of course, such a thing as a morality of institutions and groups, and early in his career he devoted a great deal of his attention to the ethics of the church. But Niebuhr has always assumed that morality is primarily located in the experiences and relationships of the feeling, thinking, deciding *self*, and this priority is clearly evident in his teaching and writing over the last twenty years of his life. This concentration on the responsible self does not involve an ethics of individualism or voluntarism. The moral actor is not the isolated individual choosing his own destiny or determining his own duty. Rather, moral transactions are the actions of a fully historic and social self responding to God and neighbor in concrete situations of interaction. Thus Niebuhr's ethics of radical monotheism concentrates on exploring the distinctive features, patterns and strategies of responsibility in the lives of confessing Christians.

FEATURES OF RADICAL RESPONSIBILITY

We have seen above that all moral action exhibits a general structure of responsiveness, interpretation, accountability and social solidarity. Every moral agent is responsive and accountable in the light of some communally shared understanding of human life and meaning. But particular persons may and do differ over what they are responsible *to* and accountable *for* when they live out of fundamentally different communities. Every community of moral interaction develops a distinctive understanding of its own center and scope of responsibility.

Thus, for example, a racist community lives by an ethics that extends the sense of human worth and individual duty no farther than the boundaries of the "super race." A humanistic ethics includes all persons in the circle of moral care, because the family of man is the source and sum of human good and obligation. But humanism finds no such value or duty in the inanimate and animate milieu that encompasses human life. In contrast to all such ethics with finite centers and circles of value, the ethics of radical monotheism is theocentric and universalistic.

The primary and pivotal feature of Niebuhr's ethics is its *theocentrism.*[1] As he so often does, Niebuhr partly defines his own position by contrasting it with other stances. Theocentric ethics is clearly different from systems of morality which define goodness and obligation in finite terms such as personal pleasure (hedonism), social welfare (utilitarianism), self-preservation (vitalism) or rational consistency (formalism). But God-centered ethics must also be distinguished from those "specious surrogates" which often pass as theocentric because of their close association with the way radical faith arises.[2] Because God is known only through historical mediators and fallible authorities, there is always the danger for Christians of substituting the authority of the church, the teaching of the Bible or the dictates of conscience for God. Again and again, Niebuhr warns, those who bear the name of Christ put their trust and loyalty in fallible mediators and authorities rather than looking through and beyond them to the infallible God they reveal. But church-centered, Bible-centered, or conscience-centered ethics are no less a denial of theocentrism than those which center in the body, the mind, the state, or the earth. Indeed, sometimes they are more a perversion of Christian ethics than such secular moralities.

In contrast, the ethics of radical monotheism centers in no finite being or value. To drive this point home, Niebuhr is critical of even speaking of God as Being or as the Good. That way of characterizing the transcendence and sovereignty of God too easily lends itself to equating God with the whole of finite being and value. But God for Niebuhr is no more the whole than some part of the finite universe. Pressing for optimum clarity he writes:

> I use the terms "principle of being" and "principle of value" in distinction from the terms "highest being" and "highest value," or "Being" and "the Good," because the principle of being is not immediately to be identified with being nor the principle of value with value. As many theologians have undertaken to say, "God is beyond being" they ought also to say that he is beyond value.[3]

The ethics of radical monotheism is that mode of life centered exclusively in God who is the source and the norm of all being and value.

In Niebuhr's theocentric ethics, God does not stand at the center of the moral life as the Lawgiver for a kingdom of subjects (deontological ethics) or as the Plan Maker for a team of builders (teleological ethics). Rather, God himself is at the center of morality as the Primary Agent in a community of agents, as the First Person in a society of persons.[4] In the response ethics of Christian faith all moral action is a human reaction to divine action. The human *imperative* always arises out of the divine *indicative*. Moral obligation is always a matter of making fitting response to what God is doing in a concrete situation of divine-human interaction. Thus, rephrasing Kant, Niebuhr sums up Christian ethics in one categorical imperative: "God is acting in all actions on you. So respond to all actions upon you as to respond to his action."[5]

What then is God doing that requires our response? For Niebuhr, any answer to that question must hold together the power and the goodness of God. God's action cannot be somehow divided such that his power is operative and his goodness is realized only for certain people and special events. God's action must ultimately be the one power behind and within all things, and that action must always be benevolent. Despite all doubt and suspicion, suffering and failure, responding to the action of God upon us means becoming responsible to and responsible for a radically inclusive community of being and value.

The second distinctive feature of Niebuhr's ethics, following directly from theocentrism, is *universalism.* An ethics of response to the one God acting in all times and places is necessarily all-inclusive in its scope. The God at its center bestows value on *all* things, enjoins community with *all* things, and requires responsibility for *all* things.

In Niebuhr's ethics, values are centered in God but they are not limited to God. To the contrary, a God-centered ethics *must* acknowledge the value of all things, since things have value in relation to God and God is always related to all things. Value for Niebuhr is always a relational property.[6] Worth and meaning do not inhere in things or persons. Rather, value arises and endures only in reciprocal relationships of being good *for* another and of receiving good *from* another. Dangerous as it sounds, Niebuhr apparently maintains that neither God nor man has value in himself, but each has value in relationship to the other.

There is, of course, a difference in the values that arise within finite relationships and those that derive from the Infinite God. Man's value relationships are derivative while God's are generative. God bestows value on all finite things and interrelationships by sustaining a relationship with them. This means that divinely bestowed value is never absent, though it is seldom present in a positive way. Put in Niebuhr's technical terminology: "To say that this faith acknowledges whatever is to be good is not to say, of course, that for it whatever is, is right." [7] Not all things are in right relationship to one another or to God, but their real and potential goodness remains fundamentally intact because they are still related to God. Reserving infinite worth for God is the very means of preserving the finite worth of all things.

God's universal bestowal of value creates a universal community of valued and valuing beings.[8] In the same way that he contrasts theocentric ethics with ethics having lesser value centers, Niebuhr separates the ethics of universal community from those that are less inclusive. In fact the quickest way to discover whether an ethics is theocentric is to determine whether it en-

joins a genuinely universal community. Against all ethics of
the "closed society," Niebuhr maintains: "When I respond to
the One creative power, I place my companions, *human and
subhuman and superhuman,* in the one universal society which
has its center neither in me nor in any finite cause, but in the
Transcendent One." [9]

Lest there be any misunderstanding of the radical inclusiveness of this society, he elaborates on this theme in a number
of contexts. For the morality of radical faith, the "neighbor in
being" includes the near and the far, the believer and the unbeliever, the friend and the foe, the living and the dead, the
animate and the inanimate, the real and the ideal, the macro-
cosmic and the microscopic.[10] In eloquent summary: "He is
man and he is angel, and he is animal and inorganic being, all
that participates in being." [11]

Membership in this universal community requires responsibility for *every* neighbor in being.[12] Niebuhr variously describes
the meaning of such universal accountability. Philosophically,
responsibility for the neighbor is a matter of seeking and
sustaining a universal network of *right* relationships—those relations between beings in which their potential for being "good-
for" and "good-from" each other is realized.[13] In more personal
and lyrical language, Niebuhr identifies universal responsibility
as loving every neighbor in rejoicing and reverence, in gratitude
and loyalty.[14] As we shall see presently, such love does not rule
out limiting, disciplining and even fighting the neighbor. Whatever the terminology, Niebuhr is clear that the ethics of radical
faith creates a universal brotherhood of brother's keepers.

Niebuhr thus defines the distinctive meaning of responsibility
for radical monotheism in terms of theocentrism and universalism. No clearer statement of these features could be wanted than
Niebuhr's assertion: "Radical monotheism dethrones all absolutes short of the principle of being itself. At the same time it
reverences every relative existent. Its two great mottoes are: 'I
am the Lord thy God; thou shalt have no other gods before me'
and 'Whatever is, is good.' " [15] Here in capsule form is the
whole intent and content of the ethics of radical monotheism.

But such distilled formulations of moral responsibility do not furnish the kind of interpretive framework required for making concrete decisions in concrete situations. We need fuller understanding of the patterns of divine action and human response in order to interpret each circumstance of life as a moral interaction with God and neighbor.

PATTERNS OF DIVINE ACTION

For Niebuhr morality is a matter of "fitting response" to God's action upon us in and through our interactions with the neighbor.[16] The concept of "fittingness" emphasizes the contextual and interpretive character of all moral responses. The moral agent must decide what actions fit or do not fit in a given situation. His response cannot be prescribed or guaranteed beforehand by some set of moral norms or case studies. A moral response must fit the occasion like a "sentence fits into a paragraph in a book, a note into a chord in a movement in a symphony, as the act of eating a common meal fits into the lifelong companionship of a family, as the decision of a statesman fits into the ongoing movement of his nation's life with other nations, or as the discovery of a scientific verifact fits into the history of science." [17]

This means that Niebuhr, like other so-called "situation ethicists," believes that the imperatives for particular decisions are derived from the indicatives of particular situations. Moral obligation must be determined afresh in every concrete situation of divine and human interaction. But, unlike some situationalists, he does not determine what God is doing in a concrete situation by appealing to an intuitive grasp (Bishop Robinson) or to a casuistry of love (Joseph Fletcher). Instead, Niebuhr makes use of certain *patterns* of divine action and human response to interpret what God is doing and requiring in a particular situation. Niebuhr's appeal to such patterns is not a denial of the relativities of every moral decision. He insists on the necessity of wrestling with situational contingencies and

novelties in all moral deliberation and decision. Rather, he
employs such patterns as the informing and inspiring *images*
of moral reflection. Niebuhr's religious and moral responses to
God are always informed by *imaginative* reasoning—by order-
ing and interpreting human experience in and through selected
images and imaginings. Thus, he appeals to patterns not to
escape but to engage the particularities of a situation of moral
interaction.

What then are Niebuhr's interpretive patterns of moral responsibility? Certainly the central pattern in Niebuhr's published materials is christological. He makes frequent use of the
moral "paradigm of Christ"—his vicarious suffering, his
resolute faith, his God-centered virtue.[18] But those who studied
with Niebuhr know that in his systematic ethics lectures he
regularly used a trinitarian pattern for interpreting moral responsibility. Moral action is a response to what God is doing
as the Creator, Judge and Redeemer of all things.

Before discussing this threefold pattern, several cautions
should be kept in mind. First, Niebuhr's use of a basically
trinitarian model is no concession to the binding authority of
biblical or creedal trinitarianism. He makes use of trinitarian
categories because they make sense out of moral life today.
Second, Niebuhr does not apply the categories of Creator, Judge
and Redeemer as chronological sequences or dispensational
eras—as if God first creates, then judges, and finally redeems
the individual or the world. God's action is one in all times and
places, but that single action is always simultaneously creating,
judging and redeeming the world. Third, though there is no
chronological or sequential order in these three aspects of
God's activity, there is a "logical" order. Redemption has
priority in Niebuhr's thinking over creation and judgment. Indeed, we only understand the true nature of our being and
value, as well as our limitations and sufferings from within
the standpoint of God's revelation and reconciliation in Jesus
Christ. All that Niebuhr has to say about *natural* religion
and morality is derived from the standpoint of *radical* faith and
responsibility. Thus, his understanding of God's creative and

judging action follows from his interpretation of God's redemptive action, even though in his lectures on this threefold pattern
his discussion of redemption always comes last. With these
cautions in mind, we shall now examine Niebuhr's understanding of morality as fitting response to God's action as Creator,
Judge and Redeemer.[19]

Niebuhr builds an "ethics of world affirmation" on the action
of God as Creator.[20] His interpretation of God's creative activity does not deal with when or how or why the world came to
be. Rather, his "doctrine of creation" explains the fundamental
nature and consequences of God's relation to the world in every
place and in every time. By virtue of God's continuous and
creative work in the world, the whole of creation is knowable,
purposive and good.

Behind Niebuhr's view of the creative action of God stands
his relational value theory. As we saw above, all values arise in
relationships of "good-for-ness" and "good-from-ness." All
things derive their worth in dependence upon and in service to
those manifold others ("human, subhuman and superhuman")
with which they interact. But such relational worth has no
integrity or endurance apart from a transcendent "center of
value" that conveys goodness to all things and requires rightness
in all relationships. For Niebuhr, God is that center of value
who creates and sustains a universe that is radically good—in
whole and in all of its parts.

Man's fitting response to such creative action of God is radical "world affirmation." But this response is possible only
within radical faith. The vast majority of our finite relationships
are anything but right, and the One Power behind and in all
things seems more like a Destroyer than a Creator to the eyes
and faith of natural man. But in the revolution of life that
comes with radical faith, these attitudes and ideas about ourselves and our total environment begin to change. In fact, Niebuhr sees five stages in this transformation of our responses to
the value of God and of God's creatures. First, there is *acceptance* of our existence and of the right to be of all things.
This initial stage is followed by the *affirmation* that "what is,

ought to be" because God can be trusted to bring some good from failed relationships as well as successful ones. The third stage in our response to God as Creator is *understanding* how things are in their marvelous order and terrifying disorder. Such "thinking the thoughts of the Creator after him" facilitates the *cultivation* of God's creatures and creation by judiciously and sympathetically seeking and receiving their true good. Finally the highest stage of response to God is *imitation* of his creative work by sharing in the ongoing achievement of novel goods and harmonious relationships.

In sketching out these levels of faithful response to the Creator God, Niebuhr does not lose sight of the difficulty and even tragedy that accompanies such responses. He is aware that the resolve to respond to God as life's Infinite Value does not automatically settle the tough problems of deciding between life's finite values and valuers. Though in faith all things may be affirmed as equally good for God and from God, we must in practice choose between goods—prefer this person above that, honor this claim rather than the other, preserve this group against that. How can we arbitrate concrete problems of value preference and value conflict?

Niebuhr offers no simple, foolproof formula for choosing between greater and lesser goods, but he does offer three helpful guidelines. First, do not prefer yourself over others because "you are being loved by God and by your neighbor; therefore, you do not need to practice self-love." [21] The second principle for deciding preferences is to serve that value which is in greatest need of your service rather than what is rightly considered highest. Finally, serve not only the neediest but also the nearest at hand. Following these rules will in no way enable us to eliminate the sacrifices and suffering that all our choices will require, but we can act on them out of the confidence that we live in a universe where vicarious suffering can be creative rather than destructive because God binds up and heals all wounds. Ultimately the responsibility to make good such imperfect though well-meaning responses is his alone.

Implied and present in this view of the creative action of God is the recognition that though "whatever is, is good" not "everything that is good, is right." Life in God's good world is disordered and deranged by wrong relationships and wrong preferences. We serve ourselves above others, we love our friends to the exclusions of our foes, we trust in finite things rather than God. For Niebuhr, this means that God's action in the world exhibits a pattern of judgment as well as creation. But, as we shall see, God's judging action only restrains in order to redirect the misuse and abuse of his good creation.

Niebuhr develops an "ethics of limitation" in response to God's governance of the world.[22] Life in God's good world is no idyll of freedom and harmony. More typically, we suffer and inflict experiences of limitation and disintegration. We are, in Niebuhr's words, "killed all the day long." But these experiences must be understood as expressions of God's creative and redemptive purposes if world affirmation and transformation are to make any sense.

Niebuhr begins his "ethics of limitation" with a discussion of those limitations which, as permanent features of creaturely existence, are the perennial sources of misery and want. We are always limited *physically* as embodied beings needing space and support from the physical environment and suffering competition and attack from other embodied beings. We are limited *mentally* by the reach and relativity of our powers of mind to understand ourselves and our world. We are limited *socially* by only having life in and through bounded groups which, though larger and stronger than ourselves, are also caught in the conflicts and failings of all things finite. All these limitations press in upon us causing pain, as we in turn press upon others causing them pain. Out of this struggle with limitations and impingements, we typically create divisions and erect defenses. Our world is fractured into ally and enemy, in-group and out-group, friend and stranger, and we assign correspondingly separate schemes of values and rights to these divisions.

Niebuhr believes that radical faith can interpret these experiences of limitation and antagonism by a different pattern—monistic rather than dualistic, conciliatory rather than divisive.

He perceives in these very experiences the action of one Power who limits and even destroys finite things and relationships for the sake of their ultimate renewal and completion. He interprets the very conditions of limitation, which men think are the sources of all evil and death, as the structures of well-being and life. God the Judge governs his world through the finite and mutual dependence of men upon one another in such a way that each is aided as well as restricted by the other. Such reciprocity is never achieved apart from conflict and suffering.[23] Indeed, God's world is an order of vicarious suffering and undeserved success. The innocent bear the sins of the wicked and the fortunate prosper at the expense of the deserving. Life and history lend no support and sustain no hope for a neatly proportional distribution of rewards and punishments. But God's governing action weaves the lives and deeds, the gains and losses of all into the good for each and the good of all.

As already indicated, this way of perceiving the oppressive conditions and experiences of life makes sense only to radical faith. Seeing God at work in the structures of suffering in this manner, Niebuhr suggests two fitting responses.[24] One is the response of *self-denial*. This does not mean the negation of the self in penance or compensation for one's own shortcomings. Instead, it means taking the triumphs and losses we undergo in an "impersonal" way since we are never specially or personally marked out for favor or for punishment. Self-denial further means the acceptance of all experiences of limitation as reformatory. While none of life's limitations are visitations of arbitrary punishments, many are the outcome of our idolatrous loves and loyalties. The dissolution of such wrong priorities and relationships, with all the attendant suffering that results, can lead life to reformation. Finally, a response of self-denial means accepting our limitations vicariously as the price to be paid for living in an interdependent and imperfect community of finite beings and values.

A second fitting response to God's governing action, sometimes more difficult to manage than self-denial, is the *restraint of others*. In the confidence that conflict can be creative and renewing, the faithful must restrain the neighbor's egoism and evil. Passive nonresistance may be a fitting response of an individual to his own aggressors, but it is never a morally responsible way of dealing with aggression by a third party against one's neighbor. We are obligated to restrain evil in others for *their* sakes as well as for our neighbor's and our own. But in limiting and disciplining others, we must always affirm their fundamental goodness and seek to realize that basic goodness in and through renewal of relationships between us. This means that controls and constraints, disciplines and penalties must always be humane and medicinal, which in turn means that they must never *will* the other's destruction. Above all, response to the Judge by restraining others must always be undertaken in the full recognition that such actions are themselves imperfect and thus need the restraint of others. As Niebuhr succinctly puts it, "Christian restraint is the restraint of sinners by sinners." [25]

Such positive and creative responses to limitation can mean a new beginning for our lives and the lives of others. The God who appears in this judgment of the world is neither the amiable parent of the soft faith of liberalism nor the vengeful deity of the harsh faith of orthodoxy. He is the eternal Creator, Judge and Redeemer "whom prophets and apostles heard, and saw at work, casting down *and* raising up." [26] In other words, God's action is all of one piece. To discern God active in judgment is to see God destroying our idols of self-confidence and our hells of self-isolation, redemptively driving us to recognize our sole dependence upon him to renew individual worth and to reestablish cosmic community. To complete Niebuhr's picture of God's total action, then, we must consider God's action as Redeemer.

Niebuhr's final and definitive pattern of divine action and human response centers in God's action as Redeemer. This third image actually expresses the whole sum and substance of God's work in the world. The worth of the whole universe can be joyously affirmed only when we know that the Power in and beyond all things is good. Life's limitations and losses can be graciously accepted only when we know they do not ultimately destroy or separate us from God's universal community. In a word, an "ethics of renewal" stands at the heart of Christian faith and radical monotheism.

From the first pages of this study, we have seen that *metanoia* is the one term that Niebuhr constantly uses to characterize God's action and man's response. He freely employs many synonyms for this Greek word meaning "change of mind"— repentance, conversion, redemption, republication, reinterpretation, revolution, reconstruction, restoration, reorganization, metamorphosis, transformation, transvaluation, transfiguration.[27] But running through all is a sure sense of God's active *movement* in our world and man's active *change* in response to God.

Before discussing man's response to this redeeming movement, two reminders are worth mentioning. First, for Niebuhr there is no gradual and progressive achievement of redemption in human history or individual existence. New levels of life and depths of insight have emerged in God's redemptive dealings with the world, but these are not neatly cumulative or successive. Every advance carries with it new opportunities and propensities for faithlessness and barbarism. At work in every time and place is God's creating and judging as well as his redeeming action. A second reminder is that God's redemptive action is not limited to Christian history or Christian revelation. While Christians must refrain from imposing their theological and moral categories on the whole of human history, they are also forbidden to deny that the God revealed in Jesus Christ is the universal Lord of heaven and earth. Christians are therefore compelled to respond to all events and actions as the work of that One God whose redeeming action includes all companions in being (whether "human, subhuman or superhuman").

What, then, are fitting responses to God's movement of renewal in and through, for and by all things? Response to God's redeeming action means appropriating and participating in that work of God which is understood in and through Jesus Christ as aggressive love and vicarious suffering. Sharing in God's renewal of all things means willing and working for the integrity

and community of all things—helping each fulfill its potential-
ity in mutuality with every other as far as possible, even at the
cost of suffering for ourselves and others. Focusing more concretely on personal and social responsibility, an "ethics of
renewal" calls on us to rethink all our past history, present experience and future expectations in the light of God's "permanent revolution" in the world. This means weaving every
incident in internal and external history, every facet of personal and public life together into one fabric. Sharing in God's
work of renewing and reconciling all things means *representa-
tively* repenting and reconstructing the world's loves and loyalties. As genuinely difficult as these responses of rethinking and
redoing life are, Niebuhr contends they are made possible by
radical faith's assurance that ultimately God works in us and
gives us the victory.

This description of the trinitarian patterns of God's action
typifies how Niebuhr reasons about moral matters. Situational
responses to God are not based on intuitive or principled deter-
minations of what God is doing in that situation. The will and
the work of God are not discerned in immediate encounter nor
enshrined in universal principles. But Niebuhr does insist that
we can and do personally encounter God in situations of moral
interaction by interpreting those situations as God's action on
us as Creator, Judge and Redeemer. Elaborating on these
images, Niebuhr teases out the kinds of questions and attitudes
that guide the discovery of "what is going on" and "what will
fit in" in concrete situations. But Niebuhr encourages the use of
other interpretive resources for coming to decisions than these
heuristic patterns alone. In fact, he welcomes the strategic use
of any account and guide of the moral life so long as it is
brought under and into a theocentric and universalistic vision of
morality.

STRATEGIES OF MORAL DECISION

For Niebuhr, response to the triune God does not require the
repudiation or abandonment of existing relationships and pre-

vailing morals, but instead their "criticism and reconstruction." [28] As we have seen, radical faith is not the completion or the destruction of man's natural faith but its thoroughgoing transformation. By the same measure, radical morality is not the ratification or the repeal of man's natural morality but its radical transvaluation. [29] This transvaluation is a process of bringing all moral action and reflection under a theocentric and universalistic sense of moral responsibility. This process does not lead to a single abstract and encompassing system of Christian ethics. To the contrary, a theocentric and universalistic ethics permits and requires many relative value systems—each of them tentative and restrictive in how they view moral interaction and responsibility but each helpful in bringing to light the operative facts and values in a concrete situation. The Christian moralist needs all the help he can get in understanding the structures of personal and institutional relationships within which he acts. He needs to be aware of the belief systems and value schemes that lie behind individual and group behaviors. He needs to understand proximate ends and likely consequences for various courses of actions. The more the Christian ethicist can learn about the actions and interactions at work in a moral situation, the greater his ability to bring to light their real trusts and loyalties and turn them toward a theocentric universalism.

Happily, Niebuhr contends, the ethics of radical monotheism is not required to construct such multiple and perspectival accounts of human behavior and moral guidance. A wealth of such systems are at hand in the West's long tradition of philosophical ethics, both Christian and non-Christian. Here are readily available analyses of principles and ideals, motives and consequences, duties and rights, virtues and values, freedom and obligation, conscience and authority, guilt and punishment. All these differing approaches to the central themes and typical dilemmas of ethical reflection can be useful in shaping social policy and situational decisions *if* they are brought under the critique and put to the service of radical faith.

How this reconstructive appropriation of varied and conflicting ethical schemes proceeds is suggested by Niebuhr's own work. His lectures on ethics are a running dialogue with virtually every major moral philosopher on the central problems of ethical theory. His theological and ethical writings reflect this same lively conversation with other viewpoints. Frequently and typically Niebuhr plays off the strengths and weaknesses of opposing points of view as a way of moving toward a more satisfactory position that takes up their respective strengths and avoids their weaknesses.

This dialectical style is especially evident in his two major statements on morality. *Christ and Culture* is a subtle argument for the "conversionist" view of the Christian relation to cultural life. Niebuhr moves from the untenable extremes of Christian opposition and Christian accommodation to culture through two unsatisfactory attempts to relate Christian faith and cultural life hierarchically or paradoxically, finally arriving at the more adequate approach wherein the Christian seeks to transform his culture.

The Responsible Self not only advocates "responsibility" as a new alternative to the more venerable theories of "teleology" and "deontology"; the entire book is a deft exercise in alternately recasting teleological and deontological approaches in terms of responsibility or drawing on them as ways of deepening and clarifying the meaning of responsibility. There is no intended deception or pretension in this for Niebuhr. This way of thinking and proceeding is the way of *metanoia,* the strategy of conversionism—to relate and refine and renew one's own understanding through reformulating all the wisdom of men in light of the wisdom of God. Radical faith can draw on and learn from the partial insights and necessary conflicts of all serious accounts of the moral life by bringing them under its vision of one exclusive center of responsibility and one inclusive circle of accountability.

Having seen how Niebuhr's ethics *can* devise principles of action and strategies of decision in concrete situations by critically clarifying and revising existing ethical systems, we must now note that Niebuhr does little of this in his teach-

ing or his writing. He seldom gets down to actual cases of re-
solving specific moral problems through the application of
specific moral reasoning. In the few published articles where he
addresses a specific problem, such as the celebrated exchange
with his brother over how Christians should respond to the Sino-
Japanese conflict, he focuses more on what God is doing in
those situations than upon what man ought to do in response.[30]
His major ethics course at Yale always included a lengthy
section in the syllabus on particular problems of responsibility
within the central communities of the common life—domestic,
economic, political and religious.[31] But the surviving transcripts
of these lectures indicate that he seldom dealt with these concrete issues in any depth or thoroughness. Whether this failure
was the result of the professor's perennial problem of "finishing
the outline" is hard to say. But the fact remains that we have
little indication of how Niebuhr's ethics finds specific principles
and warrants for action in a specific situation.

This absence of casuistry is considered a serious weakness in
Niebuhr's ethics by some of his closest followers as well as his
sternest critics. Niebuhr does seem a better architect than
engineer of moral behavior. He draws with compelling beauty
and plots with discerning precision the faith-context of moral
action in general and Christian moral action in particular. This
enables him to critically evaluate the real trusts and loyalties
that underlie typical moral communities and actions and equips
him to constructively commend the advantages of a theocentric
and universalistic understanding of moral responsibility by ex-
posing the limitations of these lesser moralities. But Niebuhr's
critical and constructive handling of other moral viewpoints remains largely at the *metatheoretical* level—at the level of
defining key categories and establishing the fundamental standpoint and scope of ethical reflection. Niebuhr's actual "conversion" of systems of ethics that are not radically theocentric
and universalistic seldom goes beyond breaking them open to
this more transcendental and global locating of morality. He
does not, in fact, use them as the materials at hand for building
specific guidelines for personal action and social policy.

Without prosecuting or acquitting Niebuhr on this charge, I should like to make four points. First, even at the generalized level of analyzing the structures and essentials of responsibility, Niebuhr's ethics is not bereft of normative content and concrete guidance. Niebuhr would contend that ethicists, Christian and non-Christian alike, have overstressed the importance of rational deliberation and formal principles in moral action. Assumptions about how things are and ought to be, of course, do underlie moral action and these need to be brought to awareness for clarification and reformulation in ethical inquiry. But these assumptions in real life are more context-encompassing than situation-specific. They articulate the context for any decision rather than catalog in computer fashion the rules of every decision. Nevertheless these context-encompassing assumptions are value-laden and hence sanction only certain kinds of specific responses.

Second, even in the use of patterns of divine action, whether trinitarian or christological, Niebuhr's ethical reflection is not lacking normative content and behaviorial directives. Niebuhr's stress on the central role of images in thought and paradigms in conduct carries with it the recognition that symbols have cognitive and conative power as well as emotional force. Most moralists have been tardy in recognizing what theologians, philosophers and literary critics (to say nothing of teachers, artists and prophets) have come to understand—that symbols are the primary carriers of human thought, shapers of human action, and movers of human feeling. An ethics of response guided by parables and models may be far more formative, informative and reformative than an ethics of prescriptions and exceptions.

Third, perhaps there are good reasons internal to Niebuhr's ethical system for not setting down concrete moral guidance in book fashion. Such publications invite, if not demand, being read as authorized prescriptions of moral responsibility without regard to the relativities and novelties of concrete situations of moral action. Niebuhr's reluctance to give concrete guidance may have been a consequence of his deep sense of the *per-*

manent revolution at the heart and in the midst of all things.

This possibility suggests a fourth and final characteristic of Niebuhr's approach to making actual decisions in actual situations. His own vivid sense of a God who really *is* creating, judging and redeeming *our* world and *our* lives doubtless carries a powerful sense of normative definiteness and situational fittingness in situations of moral action. Elaborate schemes of guidance likely seem unnecessary if not detrimental to him, since in the last analysis moral action means personally responding to the *God* of radical monotheism rather than to someone's beliefs about radical monotheism. Only in response to God is our responsibility for the neighbor determined and discharged.

However one assesses the strategic usefulness of Niebuhr's ethics at the level of concrete moral action, there can be no doubt that he calls persons and communities to such action. His early counsels to moral inaction and monastic withdrawal were themselves strategic moves rather than programmatic policies and even these he later saw to be ill-advised and ineffective. Throughout his long career of teaching and writing, Niebuhr summons the believer and the church to participate in God's perpetual revolution by incarnating radical faith in a life of radical responsibility.

IX. The Responsible Church

We have seen how Niebuhr conceives of the dimensions and duties of radical responsibility in the lives of selves. We must now look briefly at what such responsibility means for communities, especially for the church.

Niebuhr brings the critical and constructive powers of radical morality to bear on a number of the large institutionalized communities which daily affect the lives of individuals and groups within and beyond their borders. In his published writings he deals only with the meaning of radical responsibility in the human communities of political democracy, modern science, higher education and the Christian church.[1] With the exception of the church, Niebuhr's accounts are sketchy, but they are quite suggestive of what responsible democracy, responsible science and responsible education should be.

Niebuhr's concentration on the church should not be misunderstood. He does not think the church is somehow more religious than these other institutions of the common life. While there are indications that early in his career Niebuhr thought of the church as a very special institution, we have seen how he has progressively preferred to speak of the church as one human society among others which gives expression to faith, both nat-

ural and radical. We have also seen how again and again Niebuhr warns against the church making special claims for itself
or its revelations. Such self-aggrandizing and self-defensive
claims are henotheistic distortions of radical faith.[2] But placing
the church among other human communities and censuring its
lapses into false faith are not intended to belittle or eliminate
the importance of the church. Niebuhr does believe the church is
different from other social bodies. The church, unlike other
human communities through which God also works, is *directly*
concerned with being responsible and accountable to God. Trust
in and loyalty to God is the explicit rather than implicit raison
d'être of this particular community's life. Thus, the church has
a special function but no special character.

This distinctive function is implied in Niebuhr's greater attention to the reformation of the church over other human communities. His concentration on the church is a strategic matter.
He has always believed that Christians are responsible for the
renewal of church *and* world, but he recognizes differences in
priorities. He notes with gratitude those theologians (including
his brother) devoted to the reformation of culture, but Niebuhr
numbers himself among those who are particularly concerned
with the reformation of the church.[3] He believes the times call
for the aggressive love and dramatic example of a responsible
society as well as responsible selves. Therefore, Niebuhr summons the church to become the *responsible* church by recover-
ing its moral integrity, polar nature and revolutionary task.

THE CHURCH AS MORAL PROBLEM

As noted above, Niebuhr rejects all intentional separations of
personal and social ethics.[4] He does not deny that distinctions
can and should be made between the individual and the social
in moral reflection. One such important distinction is when one
acts representing only oneself and when one acts representing
some group. A second distinction is when one acts on another
individual and when one acts on a group. Different considera-

tions and problems arise in these different kinds of interaction. But Niebuhr finds all translations of these distinctions into different *sets* of morality pernicious. Such frequently heard claims that interpersonal relationships are governed by one kind of morality (such as love), while social relations are regulated by another (such as justice), and social offices by still another (such as corporate profits) are a denial of moral integrity and responsibility. They fragment the moral self into many selves and the moral community into many communities by shattering morality's one center and circle of responsibility. Thus Niebuhr contends against all intentional separation of individual and social responsibility. The responsible self must act out of *one* interpretive and faithful scheme of responsibility, whether he acts for himself or for a group, whether he interacts with another person or with an institution.

These distinctions do, however, raise important moral problems that must not be minimized or ignored. What happens when groups *lose* their moral integrity? What happens when group morality conflicts with the moral integrity of its members? Niebuhr is fully aware that there are often vast differences between the morality of selves and the morality of groups, despite the fact that personal and communal wholeness requires that there *ought* not to be. Depending upon circumstances, sometimes the morality of the group is more responsible and sometimes less than the morality of its members. Some might deny this by arguing that the morality of a group is simply the focused reflection of the morality of the persons who constitute the group. There is a guarded sense in which this is true. Societies are the product of the interaction of many people and of their decisions about right and wrong. But, in a more typical sense, simply equating the group's morality with that of its living constituency is false. As Niebuhr makes clear in his discussion of historical remembering, every group persists through time and change only because the common life becomes *structured*. Constitutions are written, offices are established, procedures are routinized, customs are observed which become the requirements for entrance and goodstanding in the community. This structuring is obviously value-laden both in the sense of goods sought and obligations imposed in the common life of the group. Indeed such structuring is what embodies the distinctive *ethos* of the group—its underlying sentiments and fundamental character. In this sense, groups or societies once structured certainly have a morality that is distinguishable and sometimes contradictory to the operative morality of its own members.

Niebuhr is well aware of the moral impact on an individual human life of this necessary structuring of human groupings. He also knows how difficult it is to make changes in structures of order and office, worth and duty. But change is possible because social structures are originally the product of individuals —usually founders or reformers who forge the instrumentalities of the common life in response to challenges or threats to communal survival. But such change is usually very slow because social structures take on a life of their own, since they are *intended* to endure beyond the particular individuals who indwell and enact them. Despite the difficulties, Niebuhr does press for responsible selves to refashion the structured societies in which they live so that these too may become ultimately responsible to the One God and responsible for his one world.

This responsibility to renew the structures of all human societies includes the church—especially the church, since the reform of religion is necessary for the reform of culture. Quite apart from the member individuals, the church in Niebuhr's judgment fails to reflect radical religion and radical morality in her structured life and concerted efforts. The church's regularized offices and missions, established boards and bureaucracies, as well as her articulated theologies and ethics, cry for radical reform. The church must be newly structured and committed as a community of radical responsibility.

Niebuhr has contributed substantially to that task. A surprising number of his publications are devoted explicitly to the nature and mission of the church. His three year study of theological education done with Daniel Day Williams and James M. Gustafson sets out new forms of ministry that are more con-

sonant with the calling to radical responsibility. But Niebuhr
stops far short of offering detailed programs of communal re-
forms or pressing for encompassing ecumenical mergers. New
forms of the common life of the church will come only in time
through the concerted and conflicting efforts of many responsible selves and will doubtless be nothing like a new monolithic
and global organization of the faithful. But Niebuhr does offer
a sketch of the nature and mission of the responsible church
to inform and inspire the work ahead. He contends that the
church can only become the responsible church by becoming
again a polar reality and a revolutionary community.

THE CHURCH AS POLAR REALITY

For Niebuhr, the responsible church is a polar reality. The
church falls into self-glorifying and self-protective henotheism
whenever it relaxes or dissolves certain dynamic tensions that
constitute its very being as a distinctive religious and moral
community. In *The Purpose of the Church*, Niebuhr singles out
six polarities which the church embodies or between which it
moves.[5]

First and foremost, the church as polar reality is both *subject and object*. The church is "the subjective pole of the objective rule of God." The church is not the kingdom of God nor
does it execute the rule of God. But it is the human community
where God is apprehended, worshiped, proclaimed and imi-
tated, though none of these is ever free from human limitations
and distortions. The church is not the only human community
directed toward God nor the only one wherein God is at work
redemptively. But from the Christian standpoint, it is the only
community where God has fully revealed his reconciling nature
and revolutionary action. Therefore, the responsible church
from its limited point of view and in its imperfect way always
directs attention to the Object of its faith rather than to its subjective reception or enactment of that faith. What seems important in this polarity, Niebuhr declares, "is the distinction of
the Church from the realm and rule of God; the recognition of

the primacy and independence of the divine reality which can and does act without, beyond and often despite the church; and the acceptance of the relativity yet indispensability of the Church in human relations to that reality." [6]

A second polar feature of the responsible church is that of *community and institution.* The church is something more than organization and rites, and membership in the church is something more than engaging in common doctrines, devotions and duties. The church is a community of divine and human interaction. Yet that dynamic community of interaction persists through different times and generations of common life only by virtue of the embodiment of its shared memories and hopes in certain institutional forms. The responsible church is both a structured community and a living institution.

A third polarity is the *unity and the plurality* of the church. Drawing on the New Testament analogy of the church as one body with many members, Niebuhr affirms that every national, denominational, local and temporal church is the church by virtue of participating in the whole. Yet each is only one part that makes up the whole. "The Church is one, yet also many. It is a pluralism moving toward unity and a unity diversifying and specifying itself." [7]

Closely related with the preceding polarity, the church is also a *locality and a universality.* The church is present wherever radical faith is incarnate. This means that the church is always local because radical faith on earth is only present in fully historic and social life. But the localized church implies the presence of the universal church even when no more than two or three are bound together in radical faith. The universal church is present there because wherever radical faith is, the remembered Jesus Christ is present, and he brings with him the whole company of those who have been and who will be reconciled to God and neighbor through him.

The responsible church is also *protestant and catholic.* Niebuhr of course, does not mean that historic Protestantism and Roman Catholicism together comprise the people of God. He means that the "protestant principle" of iconoclasm and the "catholic principle" of incarnation must be held together. The church must always protest against every tendency to confuse the symbol with the reality, to confuse the God experienced with the way that experience is mediated. But equally important the church must not fail to fashion and refashion symbols and rituals, thoughts and actions which mediate God. The Infinite must always be represented in finite forms as surely as the finite forms must always be restrained from displacing the Infinite.

Niebuhr's final polarity for defining the responsible church is *church and world*. Here, as in the first polarity of subject and object, the church is one of the poles. The relation between the church and the world is polar rather than simply identical or separate because both communities live under one God and because individuals may live in each at the same time. Niebuhr alternately defines the world as those separated from the infinite God (in ignorance or mistrust of God) and as those occupied with finite things (in opposition or service to God). The world is both the community of the unfaithful called into the church and the context of the faithful sent out of the church. But in no sense is the world (as community of sinful men) ever fully out of the church, nor is the church (as community of redeemed men) ever fully out of the world. "The world is sometimes enemy, sometimes partner of Church, often antagonist, always one to be befriended; now it is the co-knower, now the knower of what the Church does not know." [8] The relations between the church and world are infinitely variable but always inseparable and important.

Each of these polar elements of the church's reality reflects radical faith's double movement of responsibility to God and accountability for God's world. This is clearly seen in the first and the last pairings where the church stands in triadic relation to God and world. Indeed, the church lives and defines itself in action *vis-à-vis* God and world. Niebuhr's other polarities are tension-structures within the church which serve to keep the church radically centered in God and concerned for the world. Thus, for Niebuhr the polar nature of the responsible church reflects the revolutionary mission of the responsible church.

THE CHURCH AS REVOLUTIONARY COMMUNITY

Niebuhr applies the same fundamental understanding of responsibility to the church as he does to selves. In fact, he first outlined his ethics of responsibility in an article that focuses on the responsibility of the *church* for society.[9] The responsible church like the responsible self is responsible only to the One God and is accountable for no less than every neighbor in being. Further the fundamental content and intent of responsibility is the same for both the self and the church—*permanent revolution*.

In the first chapter, we noted that early in his career Niebuhr drew instructive comparisons between Christianity and communism as revolutionary movements. Not only was he familiar with the writings of Marx and Engels, but he was also able to observe firsthand the practical and revolutionary power of the Communist movement during his trip to Europe and a side trip to Russia in 1930. What impressed Niebuhr about the Communist movement was neither its message nor its goals but its *strategies* of revolutionary action. He was especially struck by three aspects of that strategy—their proclamation of a theory of where history is going, their sensitivity and response to social injustice and human suffering, and their forming cell groups of revolutionary life and action. In several articles during the 1930s, Niebuhr urged the church to pursue its revolutionary calling by adopting similar strategies.[10]

Niebuhr soon left behind all explicit comparisons of Communist and Christian forms of revolutionary action. But he seems to have carried something of these strategies of political millenarianisms over into his subsequent writings on the church. The clearest evidence of their influence can be seen in "The Responsibility of the Church for Society," in which he describes

the responsible church as apostle, pastor and pioneer.[11] These
three virtually reduplicate that strategic pattern of revolutionary action.

The responsible church has an *apostolic* role to play. The
revolutionary community must proclaim the revolutionary
gospel to all men and all groups. This means bringing radical
faith's iconoclastic power to bear on all finite loves and loyalties
which divide and set persons and groups against one another.
It means calling for active repentance and positive change in
the lives of selves and communities. Most important of all, it
means announcing in unmistakably relevant terms the trustworthiness and loyalty of the One Lord of life and death who
affirms the worth, orders the relationships and renews and completes the wellbeing of all things in heaven and earth.

The responsible church must also undertake a *pastoral* work.
The revolutionary community must come to the side of the neglected and the oppressed. Proclaiming reconciliation is not
enough. The church must also be reconciled to the alienated and
the undesirable. Announcing deliverance to the captives is not
enough. The church must free men from the chains of ignorance,
poverty and disease. Such pastoral outreach must go beyond
rescuing the lost one by one. The responsible church must
combat the social sources of human misery and the corporate
expressions of human sin. "Genuine pastoral interest in individuals will always lead to such results. The Church cannot
be responsible to God for men without becoming responsible
for their societies. As the interdependence of men increases in
industrial and technological civilization, the responsibility for
dealing with the great networks of relationship increases." [12]
The church which responds to the God who not only creates,
judges and redeems men but also their societies is responsible
for the pastoral care of both.

Finally, the responsible church is a social *pioneer*. The revolutionary community has a revolutionary gospel to proclaim
and to share only if it has a revolutionary gospel to *show*. The
responsible church, Niebuhr claims, is that part of the human
community that responds first to God on behalf of all:

It is the sensitive and responsive part in every society and mankind as a whole. It is that group which hears the Word of God, which sees His judgments, which has the vision of the resurrection. In its relations with God it is the pioneer part of society that responds to God on behalf of the whole society, somewhat, we may say, as science is the pioneer in responding to pattern or rationality in experience and as artists are the pioneers in responding to beauty.[13]

Unfortunately such representative responsibility has long been obscured, especially in Protestant Christianity, by an overemphasis on individualism. But the growing recognition of the solidarity of self and society in the social sciences and in everyday urban and international life is bringing modern man back to the old Hebraic and medieval awareness of representative action.

In this representational sense, the responsible church acts on behalf of all in order to move all towards radical trust in God and radical loyalty to God's cause. The church can only lead in the social act of repentance and transformation by setting its own house in order. When social customs, economic policies, political views, property holdings and personal relationships are seen to contradict radical responsibility, the responsible church sets the pace for their reformation in society by changing them within its own life. "As the representative and pioneer of mankind the church meets its social responsibility when in its own thinking, organization and action it functions as a world society, undivided by race, class and national interests." [14] Niebuhr sees this radical demonstration of faith as the highest form of social responsibility in the church. Whenever and wherever such responsibility is being exercised, the revolutionary faith of Christ is reduplicated and the revolutionary community of his followers becomes visible.

CONCLUSION: THE ETHICS OF LIFE

In conclusion, Niebuhr introduces and undertakes a new approach to theological ethics in terms of responsibility. He frames his discussion of the Christian moral life within a general theory of moral action as a double movement of responsibility to and responsibility for some shared sense of human worth and duty. These shared schemes of moral responsibility vary widely in terms of the particular goods trusted and served in a given moral community. Most often moral communities gather around some finite love and loyalty. But moralities centering in finite goods are inherently divisive and destructive. They set man against man, community against community and all against the decline and death of all things finite. Ironically this underlying defensiveness of all natural moralities is the single greatest source of human evil and error. Every such morality can only offer a "wisdom of survival" devoted to our own and our community's self-preservation and self-aggrandizement.

But Niebuhr sees an alternative to these "ethics of death" which can reconcile man to man and community to community by placing all in an ultimate context of renewal and life. Such a morality is available in radically monotheistic faith with its trust in and loyalty to the God who is the principle of all being and value. For the ethics of radical monotheism, moral action is a matter of fitting response to God who is acting on us in and through all things. Because God's action is universal, those who respond to Him in faith become accountable for a universal community of all finite things. Because God's action is redemptive, responsible agents are summoned to the permanent reformation of their own lives and the life of the world. Thus the ethics of radical monotheism derives the imperatives of human action from the indicatives of divine action. Responsible selves and responsible church are to "body forth" God in the world as he is in them—ever affirming, governing and renewing life.

Part Four

NIEBUHR
AS
RESOURCE

X. Niebuhr's Theological Ambiguities

ASSESSING A THINKER

In the study of any man's life and thought there comes a time to ask—What has he achieved? What has he contributed? Where did he fail? How long will he last? When a theology or ethics is under such normative assessment, one of two very different approaches may be adopted. On the one hand, a given formulation of the message and life of a community of faith may be evaluated from within by measuring it against the historic revelations, sacred traditions, established accounts and contemporary experiences of that community. On the other hand, a theology or ethics may be evaluated from some position other than the faith of the thinker and his community. That outside standpoint may be one of a rival community's faith (such as a Judaic or a humanistic viewpoint) or one that is more generalized and widely shared (such as a scientific or a philosophic viewpoint). In other words, critical assessment of a given theology or ethics may proceed from either a standpoint that is fundamentally internal or one that is external to the position under review.

In the foregoing chapters I have consciously avoided either kind of evaluation of H. Richard Niebuhr's work. I have simply sought to describe his theology and ethics from *his* point of view. Of course, these chapters are my interpretive arrangement and extension of the Niebuhr materials at hand, so they are not entirely free of personal bias. Reconstructing the thought of a person as complex and original as Niebuhr from writings as unsystematic and topical as his requires critical discernment and personal judgment every step of the way. But I have tried to make these interpretive decisions about the structure and substance of Niebuhr's thought in strict fidelity to that thought. The purely descriptive character of this exposition may be somewhat obscured by the critical comparisons between Niebuhr and other thinkers which play such a prominent role in the discussion. But these comparisons are essentially reports on Niebuhr's own dialogical and dialectical engagement with these other points of view. Thus throughout the preceding discussion I have "argued" Niebuhr's point of view as rigorously and persuasively as possible. But in so doing I have sought accurate portrayal rather than expressed personal approval of Niebuhr's theology and ethics.

In this concluding section, I will go beyond objective description to offer some critical assessment of Niebuhr's achievements and contributions. This assessment will not be made on the basis of some personal or communal "orthodoxy." Rather it will be broadly philosophical in the sense that Niebuhr will be tested against himself for internal consistency and against modern consciousness for contemporary relevance. The analysis will spotlight the unresolved ambiguities and enduring contributions of his theological and ethical thought. Discussion of these matters can only be brief and suggestive but I hope a clear sense of Niebuhr's contributions as a resource for contemporary religious thought and life will emerge.

FOCUSING THE ISSUES

Niebuhr's theology is by no means free of systematic difficulties and inconsistencies. No comprehensive account of religion or morality ever entirely escapes such difficulties since reality and experience are often more complex than human thought and language can grasp. In Niebuhr's case, these inherent limitations of understanding and expression are compounded with two other features of his work as a whole. For one thing, his theological and ethical reflection is existential rather than speculative in character. Though his thought centers in God, he only speaks of God as present and known in personal and social experience. He does not generalize the experience of faith into a fully developed metaphysical system of universal and coherent categories. This means that Niebuhr lets certain *experienced* tensions and polarities stand unresolved in his thought. Such existential thinking makes critical assessment difficult since explanatory confusions must in some way be sorted out from experiential complexities.

A second feature of his work which generates internal difficulties is his avowed catholicity. Niebuhr deliberately sets out to forge a new synthesis of the message and life of faith. Indeed, one of his singular gifts and distinctive achievements is the ability to bring together opposing traditions in a way that combines their strengths and sets aside their weaknesses. But Niebuhr's polar logic and suggestive syntheses contain elements that do not always neatly dovetail. Given Niebuhr's existentialism and catholicity, the presence and persistence of unresolved problems within his thought is not surprising.

A growing secondary literature on Niebuhr has ferreted out most of the critical difficulties in his thought. Recounting those challenges and corrections in detail is neither possible nor necessary for this study. But some attention should be drawn to the major difficulties that trouble his theology and ethics. Those difficulties appear precisely at the points of Niebuhr's greatest originality and power as an interpreter of Christian faith. As we have seen, theocentrism, relativism and conversionism are at the heart of his thought. These three themes express his greatest insights but they also contain his most vexing problems.

Theocentrism

Theocentrism is the dominant theme and most distinctive feature of Niebuhr's thought. He offers a bold restatement of the absolute sovereignty of God which brings every finite thing and occurrence into the single orbit of God's affirming, governing and redeeming purposes and work. In happiness and sorrow, illness and health, peace and war, life and death, God accomplishes his good and abiding ends. The adventure of human life is to discover what God is doing to achieve these ends and to respond to that action in trust and loyalty.

We have seen the theological and ethical use that Niebuhr makes of this sweeping vision of the greatness and goodness of God. Theocentrism enables him to embrace relativism without falling victim to skepticism or subjectivism. It allows him to interpret all human experiences for Christians and non-Christians alike as moments in faith. It permits him to affirm a process of transformation at work in all cultural and personal life. It furnishes him a critical perspective from which to revise and combine diverse theological and ethical traditions. Most important of all, theocentrism offers him a transcendent focus of devotion which draws men *into* rather than *away from* the world. But these assets, successful as they are in Niebuhr's hands, are not without problems.

The integrity and concreteness of Niebuhr's theocentrism is threatened by several ambiguities. The first arises from his unharmonized conceptions of God as Absolute Power and as First Person. There is a fatefulness about God's activity when conceived as power which seems at odds with the purposiveness of God's activity characterized as personal. Niebuhr's frequent allusions to God's power carry a strong sense of an inevitable determinism totally unaffected by human wishes and human actions. There is nothing arbitrary or vindictive in the ways God exercises this power. Indeed, God's power is impartial and impersonal because it is "the actual structure of things." [1] Accordingly, Niebuhr typically characterizes man's response to God the all-determining Power in terms of acquiescence and endurance.

But Niebuhr also speaks of God in concretely personal terms as the Lord of History, dynamically active in governing and transforming the lives of persons and societies. As Faithful Self,

God's actions in and through the multiplicity of events have the character of personal integrity and purposive striving. Man's response to this all-loving Companion empowers him to be a cocreator, cogovernor, and coredeemer of God's world. Niebuhr of course maintains that these two ways of characterizing divine action and human response do not imply a dualism in God (divine wrath versus divine mercy) or in man (physical determinism versus spiritual freedom). But how these impersonal and personal categories fit together without such duality is not clear in Niebuhr's thought, especially if these categories mark a dichotomy between the God of nature and the God of history. The question of this dichotomy will appear again when we consider Niebuhr's conversionism.

Paralleling these divergent metaphors of divine action on the world are questions about the nature of God's interaction with the world. The logic of Niebuhr's personal language about God strongly implies that God participates in the sufferings of the beings dependent upon him. Reconciliation to God's trustworthiness and loyalty seems to require that God in some way takes the misery and loss of all things finite into himself. Yet Niebuhr apparently stops short of making this claim. He speaks of the "vicarious suffering" of Christ and of the "redeeming principle" in God, but these are nowhere integrally joined. This reluctance to speak of God overcoming evil by undergoing and overcoming it within himself is doubtless rooted in Niebuhr's understanding of divine power. To speak of God being acted on, much less rivaled by other powers (human, subhuman or superhuman) would appear to compromise God's radical sovereignty in Niebuhr's understanding. Recently, "process theologians" have contested this reading of sovereign power by arguing that personal power is always shared power and that sovereign power is shared but unsurpassable power. Seen in this light, God's power is unsurpassable precisely because he personally endures and persuasively reorders all misuses of power.[2] On one occasion, Niebuhr seemed to move in the direction of this conception of God's longsuffering and triumphant power. In *The Meaning of Revelation*, he writes that the true nature of the power of God is made manifest in the weakness of Christ: "His power is made perfect in weakness and he exercises sovereignty more through crosses than through thrones." But the full context of this discussion of divine power suggests that God's power is not a matter of *suffering* love but of *resurrecting* love. God's power is "the power behind and in the power of death which is stronger than death." [3] Thus Niebuhr's understanding of divine power remains closer to the older sense of impassibility and forcefulness rather than this newer sense of unsurpassability and persuasiveness. As a consequence, questions persist about how God's harsh and tender actions are fully one.

Relativism

A second distinguishing feature and strength of Niebuhr's thought is relativism. He offers a theology and ethics that fully accept the relativity of the subject and the object in all human knowing, doing and feeling. We experience the world and God from within a community whose perceptions and responses are radically conditioned by that community's past and present experience. Such communal perspectives are always historically and religiously relative. Historically there are no absolutes because of the physical, social and rational limitations of finite and sinful man. But this historical relativism reflects a deeper religious ground of relativism—there are no finite absolutes because God alone is absolute. For Niebuhr, the "logic" of radical monotheism is historical and religious relativism.

We have seen in the preceding chapters something of the critical and constructive power of this theocentric relativism. Niebuhr's full acceptance of relativism requires him to continually rewrite theology and ethics in the light of new knowledge and experience. It enables him to integrate Christian thought with contemporary scientific and historical knowledge. It alerts him to look for truth and to suspect error in every viewpoint. It reminds him to respect life's multiformity while searching out its integrity. There can be little doubt that Niebuhr's critical acuity, irenic spirit and synoptic vision owe much to his acceptance of relativism as a methodological principle of all life and thought.

But Niebuhr's relativism also has its difficulties. The greatest problem has to do with how relative viewpoints are confirmed or changed, compared or synthesized. Niebuhr's epistemology sees all human understanding as language dependent and socially determinate. How then does reality break through these conditioned categories in such a way that those very categories can be critically revised or validated? How are different symbol systems from different speech communities compared or synthesized with one another?

As we saw in the fourth chapter, Niebuhr deals with these problems by stressing the independent reality of the "objects" of experience and the social corroboration of interpretive experience within a community of fellow knowers. But doubts remain that his account sufficiently guards against the possibility of systematic error or social illusion. How can we be sure that our linguistically shaped and communally confirmed understanding corresponds in some fashion to the real world unless we can somehow get beyond our own symbol system and speech community? Such a possibility need not involve a "vertical transcendence"—getting outside our conditioned speech and standpoint by appealing to some *preverbal* or *prereflective* access to reality. But it does require a "horizontal transcendence" which systematically compares and cumulatively references different conceptions of reality. Niebuhr's announced confessionalism seems to forbid such critical and constructive comparisons between different communal and interpretive standpoints. But as I will suggest below, Niebuhr is involved in just such comparisons in his phenomenological descriptions of faith and responsibility and in his critiques of natural religions and moralities. These can be properly construed as validating arguments for radical monotheism's explanatory power, social utility and heuristic fruitfulness. Even so, Niebuhr has not made the procedures of this comparative inquiry entirely clear or consistent. Thus the philosophic character of Niebuhr's thought is subject to considerable misunderstanding.

A more practical difficulty with Niebuhr's relativism has to do with its religious basis. His great stress on God's absolute sovereignty and man's absolute dependence could stifle human initiative and urgency. The prevenience and power of God at work in all things could so relativize and minimize human action that individual achievement and heroic striving are all but lost from view. We have seen of course that Niebuhr disavows all programmatic quietism and pacifism. He makes it quite clear that trust in God requires loyalty to God's cause, that response to God entails responsibility for God's cause. But there is no mistaking that a certain air of patient waiting, hopeful endurance and even willing suffering pervades Niebuhr's thought. This tendency to inaction probably reflects Niebuhr's own deep sense of the ever-present dangers of human defensiveness and mysteries of divine purposiveness in all actions. But that caution coupled with his reluctance to provide concrete guidelines and strategies for man's response to God softens the political impact and social relevance of Niebuhr's theocentric relativism.

Conversionism

Niebuhr's third distinctive motif is conversionism which is his way of putting theocentrism and relativism together. His conviction that all life and thought is an unending process of *metanoia* involves a fundamental view of reality and a distinctive method of reflection. As an interpretation of reality, conversionism perceives the world of man endlessly shaken and shaped by a process of transformation that "does not come to an end in this world, this life, or this time." [4] Conversionism as a way of thinking employs a "polar logic" which uncovers the inner tensions between opposing points of view as a way of locating new elements of truth and forming new syntheses of understanding in a continuing process of discovery.

We have seen how Niebuhr uses this interlocking perception of reality and method of reflection to enlarge the theater of Christian responsibility and to multiply the sources of Christian reflection. No domain of human experience is excluded from the transforming presence and power of God. No expression of human understanding is devoid of some insight into that ongoing process. Working out of this vision, Niebuhr develops historical and typological patterns and connections which are masterpieces of intellectual criticism and synthesis. The conversionist substance and style of his work create a vivid and dynamic sense of human life and thought at the growing edges of meaning that lie beyond our familiar experiences and concepts.

But Niebuhr's conversionism contains certain troublesome and unanswered questions. The most pressing problem is determining *what* is changed through God's transformative action. Although he disavows any cumulative or progressive betterment of life, Niebuhr does speak of the concrete transformation of persons and communities as a present and ongoing process in history. But he offers little explanation of how this happens and what it involves. He categorically rejects all supernatural portrayals of divine action as miraculous occurrences in nature or human nature. Instead he typically speaks of the transforming work of God in connection with what events mean (inner history) rather than how they occur (external history). But what are the connections here? How are the causes and meanings of events related? Is God involved in human meanings but not in natural processes? If so, how can we speak of God as the principle of *being* as well as the principle of *value?* Niebuhr's lack of clarity about the relationships between internal and external history leaves questions over what difference God really makes in the course of events or the sufferings of men.

This same problem arises in a different way at the point of Niebuhr's conversionist method of thinking. In the sixth chapter we saw that "reasoning in faith" plays a vital role in God's transforming and reconciling work. Personal and social wholeness are not achieved apart from the reconstruction of the whole of human history and natural process into a single "story." This reconstruction is a process of interpretation based on the central images given through the revelatory event and directed toward the reconciliation of all things in one God and one people of

God. Niebuhr gives magnificent examples of this conversionist process in his historical studies and his theological constructions. His "polar thinking" traces out remarkable convergences of diverse historical movements and theological viewpoints. Niebuhr of course understands these convergences in terms of human response to divine action. But what sense does it make to speak of *God* bringing about this transformation and universalization of human meanings and relationships? Why not call them instead triumphs of human imagination? Indeed, why not regard "God" as a symbolic construct or heuristic image only? Niebuhr certainly demonstrates the power of the *idea* of God for rearranging and reassessing life's meanings and relationships. But the *reality* of God remains open to radical doubt in the absence of some account of how God is the cointerpreter of transformational thinking or the cooriginator of historical transformations.

The foregoing seem to be the major internal difficulties in Niebuhr's theocentrism, relativism and conversionism. I do not suggest however that he was unaware of these problems or that they are debilitating to his theological-ethical vision. Niebuhr knew they were there because he *lived* the sovereignty of God, the historicity of man, and the revolution of life and thought. He knew firsthand the permanent alloy of suspicious defiance and trustful loyalty toward life's ultimate context. That experienced ambivalence is reflected in his theological and ethical work. Indeed, the ambiguities in Niebuhr's thought may be as much autobiographical as conceptual. His reluctance to press for greater clarity and consistency surely owes much to his sensitivity to doubt and resistance to defensiveness in himself as well as in others. But this reticence also reflects his view that man's relationship to God and to neighbor is not primarily an affair of the intellect but of the heart and will. Explaining faith rationally no more makes it rational than shortcomings in rational explanations of faith make it illusory. Thus Niebuhr seems willing to live with unfinished thinking so long as that thinking remains close to personal and social experience and open to criticism and change.

Because of the existential character of Niebuhr's thought, these ambiguities will not seriously compromise the importance or influence of his work. Far from being a liability, Niebuhr's flawed and anguished reflection will prove attractive to those who have lost their thirst for certitude and their taste for systems. They will likely find his refreshing candor, metaphoric richness and metaphysical reserve entirely appropriate to both modern consciousness and biblical religion. Others attracted to Niebuhr's thought will be less happy with any incompleteness or inconsistency that they find in Niebuhr. But there is nothing in his thought that stands in the way of developing his polarities more completely and coherently. Such revisionary work is already under way in certain circles. Thus whatever the difficulties of his thought, Niebuhr promises to be a major resource for religious life and thought for years to come.

XI. Niebuhr's Theological Relevance

Niebuhr places a high value on relevance in theological and ethical reflection. This concern has nothing to do with certain popular perversions of relevance—that vulgar consumerism which tailors the product to the buyer's tastes or that shallow eclecticism which masks a poverty of intellectual depth. Rather, for Niebuhr relevance is simply an inescapable requirement of all reflection that addresses a particular historical and religious context. Since faith involves knowledge, theological understanding must be consistent with all that we know about ourselves and our world scientifically, historically and philosophically. Since faith involves action, ethical understanding must take account of the distinctive political and economic structures, natural and technological resources, personal and social needs that set the scene for moral action. Such relevance to the present is as important as fidelity to the past and accountability for the future. Thus we impose nothing alien on the spirit or the substance of Niebuhr's thought when we inquire about its relevance to the contemporary religious and moral situation.

What then does Niebuhr contribute to the ongoing reformation of the church and world? How relevant is his work to contemporary theology and ethics? Are there central problems of

Christian existence today which Niebuhr illumines in a distinctive way or has the intellectual and existential setting for such reflection already left him behind? These questions cannot be explored in depth here but they can be briefly answered by comparing Niebuhr's thought to the central problematic of contemporary reflection and to some of the special ways Christian thinkers are addressing that problematic. These comparisons should be sufficient to indicate the admirable prescience and enduring importance of Niebuhr's thought.

THE CONTEMPORARY THEOLOGICAL SITUATION

The contemporary context for theological and ethical reflection is defined by the increasing secularity and relativity of modern life and thought.[1] The secular outlook of modern man is radically this-worldly. The universe is no longer seen as the anteroom or the shadow of an eternal and changeless supernatural order. Rather the universe is intelligible in its own terms and meaningful in its own right. Secular man finds both the means and the meaning of his life in this world. Accompanying and growing out of this secular turn is a new sense of the interdependence and incompleteness of all human actions, institutions and ideas. This acknowledgment of the relativity of all things dispenses with all unique revelations, infallible truths and dogmatic authorities. Relative man requires nothing more than tentative judgments and limited perspectives to make his way in a changing world. This pervasive mood of secularity and relativity has undermined the otherworldly and authoritarian belief systems that have informed Western cultures for a thousand years.

The impact of secularity and relativity on Christian life and thought has yet to be effectively blunted or fully absorbed. In fact, the history of modern thought can best be understood as a succession of attempts to come to terms with secularism and relativism. This search for new foundations and forms of Christian life and thought had its beginnings over three hundred years ago, but it reached a decisive and dramatic turning point in the so-called "death of God controversy" in the mid 1960s. The significance of this controversy goes beyond the "media event" that it became, though even that played a part, since the media coverage took the problems of faith and doubt out of the seminar rooms and into the streets. The pivotal importance of this public debate is that finally *the* radical question was raised: Is it possible for Christianity to do without God in a radically secular and relative world? Is it possible for Christians to speak of God in a fully secular and relative fashion? While the public furor and dominant spokesmen at the center of that storm have faded, the question of God in a secular and relative world is far from settled.

To be sure, the nostalgic 1970s have produced a surprising backlash of revived evangelical piety and spiritual disciples within the church.[2] Ideologically these resurgent otherworldly and authoritarian orientations are diametrically opposed to the secular preoccupations and relative persuasions of modern man and modern society. But these recrudescent traditions are for the most part maintained against secularity and relativity by being interiorized and privatized. Life in the natural and social world for their devotees still operates according to the secular and relative sensibilities of the culture at large. There has been no "rebirth of medievalism"—no recovery of the synthesis of the supernatural and the natural in hierarchical order. Rather religion has been split off from all public roles, political activities, social relationships and cultural institutions that lie outside the fellowship of faith. The new evangelicals and mystics have given up on finding a way to be genuinely Christian *in* and *for* a secular and relative world. For that reason, few leading thinkers have welcomed this revival of the "old time religion." The major contemporary theologians are unwilling to encourage or enter that "religious ghetto," no matter how populous and powerful it may appear at the moment. For them, the pressing agenda for responsible and relevant Christianity on this side of the "death of God controversy" is still the problem of how to speak of God and man in a secular and relative fashion.

Given this reading of the contemporary context, Niebuhr's

continuing relevance to theological and ethical reflection is obvious. He was clearly ahead of his time in discerning the irreversibility of the secularizing and relativizing of modern life and thought. More important, he was one of the first North American theologians who sought to turn those sensibilities to positive advantage for theology and ethics. What Niebuhr understood fifty years ago was that a *revised* modern consciousness and a *revised* Christian faith could be fully compatible and mutually supportive.

Niebuhr readily admits that modern secularity and relativity have discredited traditional Christianity's supernaturalism and authoritarianism. But he insists that this process of desacralization and demystification is fully compatible with a reconceived sense of God's radical sovereignty and universality. The God who is present in everything, yet contained by nothing, can only be known and served in a this-worldly and confessional way. A radically incarnational-iconoclastic God not only permits but requires a fully secular-relative existence. Seen in this light, modern consciousness is a permanent check against an irresponsible otherworldliness and divisive exclusivism in faith. But the benefits also run the other way. Radical faith preserves the genuine secularity and relativity of modern existence by giving life a center that radically transcends all material objects, historical groups or personal relationships. Life centered in earthly and transient goods alone soon ceases to be secular or relative because those goods are soon vested with an infinite importance and absolute priority. This resacralization and remystification of finite goods is an inevitable consequence of the anxiety and aggression that permeate such "one-dimensional" existence. The real enemy of a fully worldly existence is not the rule of God but the idolatries of men. The God who at once shatters all idolatries and sanctifies all things frees life in the world from fanaticism or despair. A fully secular-relative existence is permitted and preserved by a radically iconoclastic-incarnational God.

The striking thing about this approach to the modern problematic is Niebuhr's stress on God's radical transcendence. Most

recent efforts to reinterpret faith in secular and relative terms
have drawn on new models of divine immanence. God is relo-
cated in the "depth dimension," in the "structures of consciousness," or in "prototypical human gestures." [3] Niebuhr also
affirms God's presence and power in the midst of life, but his
emphasis falls on God's transcendence. Only a God radically
beyond yet universally related to the world can maintain the
worth and well-being of all things. For Niebuhr, the radically
transcendent God is the experientially relevant God!

Niebuhr offers a distinctive theology and ethics which bring
together the axial themes of modern consciousness and historic
Christianity in critical and constructive correlation. But he offers more than just an interpretation of Christian faith that
addresses the contemporary problematic. He also has much to
contribute to the several major preoccupations of contemporary
Christian thinkers. Here too Niebuhr's response to the challenges and opportunities confronting Christian life and thought
in the latter half of the twentieth century turn out to be accurate
and durable.

CONTEMPORARY THEOLOGICAL PREOCCUPATIONS

Contemporary Christian thought is a many-splendored thing.
In the absence of dominant spokesmen and commanding systems,
an unprecedented pluralism of ways of interpreting Christian
faith are being explored. But within this surfeit of theological possibilities I find three central preoccupations—the metaphysical prospect for Christian belief, the linguistic nature of
Christian existence, and the human future in Christian culture.
These have lately come to focus in three kinds of theology—
foundational, narrative and environmental.

Foundational Theology

Foundational theology's concern is to reestablish the metaphysical grounds of Christian faith. The combined impact of
secularism and relativism have called into question both the

certitude and the content of traditional belief in God. Earlier ways of handling doubt and error by appealing directly to a special revelation or a universal rationality are no longer available. Liberalism in the nineteenth century and neoorthodoxy in the twentieth century adjusted to this loss of miraculous evidences and rational demonstrations by grounding man's knowledge and assurance of God in an experiential faith. These two traditions conceive of faith and coming to faith in very different ways, but they agree that faith neither permits nor requires philosophical or scientific confirmation. Faith's understanding of God rests on its own self-evidence. But lately many thoughtful Christians have raised questions about such appeals to faith alone. They insist that the Christian's foundational belief in God must be capable of being established on some grounds other than mere faith in God. If such grounding is not possible, then Christian theism has no defense against the radical challenges and humanistic alternatives to belief in God that were so forcefully raised in the "death of God controversy." Foundational theology is the attempt to reestablish such grounds for belief.

The challenge facing foundational theology is more than a demand to find new evidence for belief in God. A new method or style of philosophical argument is also demanded. The logical forms of the traditional arguments for the existence of God are no longer possible. Foundational theologians acknowledge that we can no longer argue *deductively* from the idea of God to the reality of God (the ontological argument) nor can we *inductively* prove the existence of God from certain universal features and assumptions about the natural world (the cosmological and teleological arguments). Some other way must be found to show that Christian theism is true by virtue of its ability to make all human experience more intelligible than any nontheistic account of those experiences.

Among contemporary foundational theologians, two very different accounts of this new method of philosophic argument are being developed. One approach, pursued in the main among Roman Catholic thinkers, has been called "The Transcendental

Method." [4] This approach argues that ordinary experiences of understanding, judging, deciding and acting will show that knowledge of God is a "co-awareness" accompanying all ordinary knowledge of ordinary things. God is the "horizon" or "background" that makes any knowing whatsoever possible. This "transcendental" discovery of God is not an inference drawn from ordinary experiences but a structure discovered in ordinary experience. As such, the God thereby discovered is both contingently and necessarily known. God is discovered within contingent experiences as the necessary condition for the very occurrence of those experiences. In other words, for the transcendental method God is coknown with any knowledge of the world.

A second new style of philosophic argument, more popular among Protestant foundational theologians, has been called "Christian Natural Theology." [5] Unlike the transcendental method, which claims to establish a universal and necessary knowledge of God, Christian natural theology accepts the relativity of all human experience and the circularity of all metaphysical arguments. This approach is called *Christian* natural theology precisely because its foundational assumptions have their origin in the history and faith of the Christian community. But it is *natural* theology in the sense that it seeks to interpret and integrate the whole of human experience and reality theistically. Christian natural theology's broad circularity is by no means an exclusive trait of religiously inspired visions of the world. Any comprehensive account of things, whether theistic or nontheistic, rests on foundational assumptions which are presupposed rather than proven, relative rather than absolute. Christian natural theology thus has as much right to present a theistic account of things as any nontheistic vision of reality. The choice between such different sets of foundational assumptions can only be argued on the basis of which developed account makes the best sense of our lives and our world.

Well ahead of many of these new experiments in foundational theology, Niebuhr developed a style of philosophic argument similar to Christian natural theology. The philosophic and apologetic character of Niebuhr's work has often been over-looked or misconstrued. His insistence that theology start with revelation and proceed confessionally has usually been inter-preted as a categorical rejection of philosophical methods. This demand *is* a rejection of all philosophical appeals to universal presuppositions or universal proofs. But Niebuhr deems such appeals inappropriate for theology because he believes there are no such assumptions or evidences. Niebuhr's rejection of this *conception* of philosophy's task does not preclude commend-ing the Christian faith on the grounds of its power to make *all* human experience intelligible. Indeed, his phenomenology of faith and responsibility and his critique of natural religion and morality are philosophic arguments in just this sense.

Niebuhr's apologetics offers an "understanding of our human life from a Christian point of view." [6] His fundamental insights and images are derived from Christian history and faith but are generalized into interpretations beyond the Christian commu-nity and Christian experiences. In *The Meaning of Revelation* for example he discusses Christian faith against a generalized account of communal and personal identity. In *Radical Mono-theism and Western Culture* he analyzes Christian faith in re-lation to problems of cultural order and disorder. And in *The Responsible Self* he explains Christian ethics in the context of a comprehensive account of moral action as response. In each instance, Niebuhr speaks to problems shared by Christians and non-Christians in terms both can understand. He thereby com-mends the Christian faith as a resource for analyzing human experience and answering human needs. His generalized ac-counts and specific applications of Christian faith are nowhere offered as proofs of the faith of radical monotheism. But they are powerful and persuasive arguments that such faith makes *reasonable* sense of human life and thought.

Two features of Niebuhr's philosophic method deserve the attention of foundational theologians today. His definition of religion in terms of *values* locates religion in a dimension of experience that is both universal and particular, personal and social. Thus he is more readily able to commend Christian faith over other forms of faith than had he chosen some less concrete definition of religion such as Schleiermacher's "feeling of absolute dependence" or Tillich's "state of ultimate concern." [7] This focus on value also furnishes Niebuhr an interactional model of faith that makes the natural and the social world an integral part of religion. This puts his foundational theology in conversation with the whole range of human and cultural concerns.

A second feature of note for continuing work in foundational theology is Niebuhr's *confessional* stance. A confessional approach does not exclude theological apologetics, but it does affect the style and the content of such reflection. Confessionalism requires every apologetic theology to admit its own historic and religious relativity. It also demands relevance to the personal and communal situation at hand. Most important of all, it excludes all defensiveness and exclusivism. Foundational theology done in a confessional way is a reasoned communication of faith rather than a rational demonstration of faith. Such an approach is not only more honest in our pluralistic world but also more effective since it draws others dialogically into the drama of man's search for meaning. In short, the valuational and confessional character of Niebuhr's thought makes his work a refreshingly concrete and winsome theological apologetics.

Narrative Theology

Theological reflection took a remarkable "linguistic turn" some twenty-five years ago.[8] Problems with the accuracy and truth of religious language have always been a concern for Christian thinkers. But only in the latter half of this century has attention to the forms and functions of religious language become a major preoccupation of theological analysis. Behind this new attention to the nature and the status of religious claims lies the modern world's rejection of the *literalistic* understanding of religious language. This rejection reached clear expression in arguments against the reality of God in the early twentieth century philosophies of existentialism and logical positivism and in the midtwentieth century death-of-God theologies. In a variety of ways, they reduced all language about God to symbolic expressions of human feelings, intentions or goals. Christian theologians were quick to respond by admitting that all religious utterances are symbolic yet insisting that these very utterances describe the reality of God in a symbolic way. These linguistic theologians differ among themselves over how best to understand this process of symbolic description. Some stress the similarities between religious language and certain kinds of scientific claims.[9] For them the theoretical constructs of science and the "God talk" of theology organize and illumine large domains of experience through the use of paradigms or models. Other linguistic theologians assimilate religious language to poetic utterance.[10] For them religious language is richly metaphoric and dramatic because it gives expression to human feeling and commitment as well as to a vision of reality. In either case, these Christian thinkers argue that religious symbols point to and communicate the reality of God.

More recently many interpreters of Christianity preoccupied with religious language have refocused their concerns to pay greater attention to the larger context of religious speaking. Isolated religious symbols, theological statements and ethical directives are not typical of the living language of faith which is *narrative* in form. Myth and parable, personal biography and communal history are the primary forms of religious speech. As a consequence the center of gravity for the study of language has shifted to religion and story. Inventive work is now being done on why stories are the primary language of faith and on how a return to stories may revitalize Christian sensibilities.

Such "narrative theology" includes a variety of interests.[11] Much attention is being given to the relation between the narrative form of the story and the narrative form of religious experience to show how both bind persons and situations, actions and consequences together in a dramatic unity. Other narrative theologians concentrate more on the way faith is evoked or communicated through specific *types* of stories—biography, parable, myth, history, novel. But these varied approaches are bound together by a common conviction that stories are the primary means of religious discernment and communication in the life of faith.

Once again Niebuhr anticipated theological developments to a remarkable degree. We have seen that he renounces all theological and historical literalism and develops a clear sense of the role of symbol and image in *all* human thinking, doing and feeling. He also understands the narrative context and phrasing of all "imagistic" thinking in matters of human identity, religious experience and moral endeavor. He clearly sees that selves and communities are constituted by "the stories of our lives." [12] Finally, Niebuhr stresses the structural similarities of stories and of faith—both are dramatic ways of connecting life's happenings in an intelligible sequence and purposive order through the use of some plot-device.

Apart from furnishing rich theoretical underpinnings for the place of stories in human life and religious experience, three aspects of Niebuhr's thought are especially relevant to those doing narrative theology today. Most important is his insistence on the priority of the *communal* story. Much of the work now being done in the area of "religion as story" reflects the individualization and privatization of religion so typical of North American culture as a whole. No doubt this is largely due to the collapse of the meaningfulness of the traditional communal story for many moderns. But Niebuhr's stress on "the story of *our* lives" reminds us that religion has a world-building and group-binding role. For him, the Christian story joins the self in community with God and every neighbor in being. Niebuhr's thought is a valuable corrective to all narrowly autobiographical and politically irrelevant exercises in narrative theology.

A second important feature is Niebuhr's stress on the centrality of controlling images in life and in story. Images are the means by which actions are distributed and conflicts resolved. Images also lend an inescapable moral tone as well as aesthetic form to stories and to lives.

Finally Niebuhr presents a distinctive narrative style of theological reflection. Unlike many narrative theologians today, Niebuhr does not *replace* theology proper with personal biography or literary analysis. He builds narrative into the very texture of theological work. His great venture in historical theology, *The Kingdom of God in America,* is a subtle and skillful interweaving of three stories—the development of American Protestantism, the development of his own theological perspective, and the movement of God in and through both. Beyond this obvious "narrative theology," all of Niebuhr's writings are exercises in communication which invite participation and enactment by his readers in a fashion not unlike a well-told story. The almost storylike concreteness and directness of Niebuhr's writing is one of the distinctive features of his technical scholarship. For these reasons, Niebuhr's thought both in style and substance has considerable relevance to narrative theology today.

Environmental Theology

The problem of the environment and the human future have reached crisis proportions in the 1970s.[13] During the 1960s there were scattered voices raised in alarm about the combined impact on the ecology of population growth and technological advance. But their warnings about the exhaustion and pollution of natural resources were largely ignored. Only recently have we come to see the impending doom that threatens not only our comfortable life style but all forms of higher life on this planet.

Although the church has not led the way, urgent appeals for a new understanding of nature and a new piety toward nature have lately come from the Christian community. This call for a new environmental theology and piety represents something more than a belated response to an emergency situation. It is a summons to active repentance for having helped create that situation in the first place. These environmental prophets within the church point out that the emergence of technology and the consequent ecological crisis have their roots in *theistic* belief systems.[14] Unlike primitive and Eastern religions, Christianity and Judaism elevate man above nature and give him dominion over it. This privileged position has inspired the rise of science and technology, both of which have increased the possibilities

of human comfort and happiness by conquering disease, multi-
plying natural resources and changing the form of human labor.
But this same privileged position lends moral and religious
sanction to the ruthless and now potentially disastrous exploitation of nature. Unless these *anthropocentric* religions are dras-
tically rethought or replaced, we are headed for ecological
catastrophe. The problem of man's future on this earth is less
a problem of technology than of theology! In frank recognition
of the theological dimensions of the ecological crisis, a growing
number of Christian thinkers are addressing this crisis with a
variety of proposals.[15] But long before there was an ecological
crisis, Niebuhr foresaw something of the difficulties and offered
a solution. The environmental relevance of his theology and
ethics is prophetic in every sense of the word.

Niebuhr's theocentric theology and ethics were developed in
critical response to the "anthropocentric" and "anthropocratic"
character of liberal theology. The displacement of man as the
center and arbiter of value by the One God is a constant theme
of Niebuhr's thought from beginning to end. Whether speaking
about revelation, faith, or responsibility, he correlates a sense
of universal community with the theocentric life. "When I respond to the One creative power, I place my companions, human and subhuman and superhuman, in the one universal
society which has its center neither in me nor in any finite cause
but in the Transcendent One." [16] Faith in the One God creates a
universal community of love and care between *all* things.

In such a universal community, wanton exploitation and ex-
travagant consumption of nature's goods is forbidden. Since
God is the center of value, man cannot preempt the value of the
animate and inanimate worlds, nor can he make their value
merely instrumental to his own. Radical faith requires reverence
for the integral worth of all things in God. This does not mean
that radical faith can avoid making choices between rival goods.
Nor does it mean that man can make no use of nonhuman goods.
But it does mean that such preferential choices will not be made
without recognizing the sacrifice and appreciating the benefit
involved. It means that man and earth will mutually enjoy the

benefits and bear the costs of their community with one another and with God. Thus Niebuhr's vision of the interrelatedness of all things offers an ecological responsibility and piety that deserves further development by those concerned with environmental theology today.

CONCLUSION: RESOURCE FOR ONGOING REFORMATION

In conclusion, as suggested at the outset of this study, nothing would disturb Niebuhr more than for his thought to become a rallying cry or an ideological center for theological and ethical reflection today. But nothing would likely please him more than to be used as a resource for the ongoing reformation of the church and world. That would enable him to give as he had received—mutual instruction and criticism of all the faithful seeking understanding.

Niebuhr offers an original and powerful resymbolization of the Christian faith. He believed that the resymbolization of the message and life of faith is a continuing task for theological-ethical reflection since these articulations of believing experience must maintain a living dialogue with faith's realities and contemporary experience. But he saw the need for resymbolization as especially urgent for our time.[17] The old phrases no longer grasp or communicate the reality of human existence before God. Thus over a forty-year career of teaching and writing, Niebuhr searched for a new conceptuality vitally in touch with the immediacies of personal existence and the exegencies of cultural experience. He fashioned a personal ministry and professional scholarship distinctively Christian yet modern, Protestant yet ecumenical, American yet global. He bequeathed that living legacy to us all—churchmen and nonchurchmen, Christians and non-Christians, theists and nontheists. He asks only that we look *through* it with him into the mystery of our existence and the meaning of our faith.

Notes

PART ONE

Chapter I

1. H. Richard Niebuhr, "Reformation: Continuing Imperative," *Christian Century* 77 (1960): 250.

2. Martin Marty surmises that Niebuhr's legacy is among the richest in American theology of the twentieth century. "Foreword" in John D. Godsey, *The Promise of H. Richard Niebuhr* (Philadelphia: J. B. Lippincott Co., 1970), p. 7.

3. Niebuhr, "Reformation," p. 248.

4. Brief biographical accounts are contained in *Faith and Ethics: The Theology of H. Richard Niebuhr*, ed. Paul Ramsey (New York: Harper & Bros., 1957), p. vii; Godsey, *The Promise of H. Richard Niebuhr*, pp. 11–19; James W. Fowler, *To See the Kingdom: The Theological Vision of H. Richard Niebuhr* (Nashville: Abingdon Press, 1974), pp. 1–8. I have drawn freely on these accounts in my own telling of his life.

5. H. Richard Niebuhr, *The Social Sources of Denominationalism* (1929; reprint ed., New York: Meridian Books, 1957).

6. H. Richard Niebuhr, "Can German and American Christians Understand Each Other?" *Christian Century* 47 (1930): 915.

7. H. Richard Niebuhr, "Translator's Preface" to Paul Tillich, *The Religious Situation* (1932; reprint ed., New York: Meridian Books, 1956).

8. H. Richard Niebuhr, "Faith, Works and Social Salvation," *Re-*

ligion in Life 1 (1932): 426–30; "Nationalism, Socialism and Christianity," *World Tomorrow* 16 (1933): 469–70; "Toward the Emancipation of the Church," *Christendom* 1 (1935): 135–45; "The Attack Upon the Social Gospel," *Religion in Life* 5 (1936): 176–81; "The Christian Evangel and Social Culture," *Religion in Life* 8 (1939): 44–48.

9. H. Richard Niebuhr, Wilhelm Pauck and Francis P. Miller, *The Church Against the World* (Chicago: Willett, Clark & Co., 1935), pp. 1–13, 123–56.

10. H. Richard Niebuhr, *The Kingdom of God in America* (1937; reprint ed., New York: Harper & Bros. Torchbooks, 1959).

11. H. Richard Niebuhr, *The Meaning of Revelation* (New York: Macmillan Co., 1941).

12. H. Richard Niebuhr, "War as the Judgment of God," *Christian Century* 59 (1942): 630–33; "Is God in the War?" ibid., pp. 953–55; "War as Crucifixion," ibid. 60 (1943): 513–15.

13. H. Richard Niebuhr, *Christ and Culture* (1951; reprint ed., New York: Harper & Bros. Torchbooks, 1956).

14. For a detailed discussion of this important unpublished manuscript, see Fowler, *To See the Kingdom*, pp. 201–247.

15. H. Richard Niebuhr, *Radical Monotheism and Western Culture* (New York: Harper & Bros., 1960).

16. H. Richard Niebuhr and D. D. Williams, eds., *The Ministry in Historical Perspectives* (New York: Harper & Bros., 1956); H. Richard Niebuhr, D. D. Williams, and J. M. Gustafson, *The Advancement of Theological Education* (New York: Harper & Bros., 1957).

17. H. Richard Niebuhr, *The Purpose of the Church and Its Ministry* (New York: Harper & Bros., 1956).

18. H. Richard Niebuhr, *The Responsible Self* (New York: Harper & Row, 1963).

Chapter II
1. H. Richard Niebuhr, "Ernst Troeltsch's Philosophy of Religion" (Ph.D. diss., Yale University, 1924).

2. For a brief account of this development, see Ernst Troeltsch, *Christian Thought* (New York: Meridian Books, 1957), pp. 35–66.

3. For D. C. Macintosh's major statement, see his *Theology as an Empirical Science* (New York: Macmillan Co., 1919).

4. D. C. Macintosh, ed., *Religious Realism* (New York: Macmillan Co., 1931), p. 376.

5. For Barth's critique of this process, see his *The Humanity of God* (Richmond: John Knox Press, 1960), pp. 11–33.

6. H. Richard Niebuhr, "Religious Realism in the Twentieth Century," in Macintosh, ed., *Religious Realism*, pp. 419–21. Barth's in-

fluence on Niebuhr's theology was primarily critical. He forced Niebuhr to go beyond Troeltsch and Macintosh. But Barth did have a direct and powerful influence on Niebuhr's strategies for church renewal in the 1930s and early forties.

7. See Paul Tillich, *The Religious Situation* and *The Interpretation of History* (New York: Charles Scribner's Sons, 1936).

8. Niebuhr, "Can German and American Christians Understand Each Other?"

9. Niebuhr, "Religious Realism," p. 428.

10. Niebuhr, "Can German and American Christians Understand Each Other?" pp. 914–16; "Religious Realism," pp. 413–28; "Translator's Preface," pp. 9–24; "Value Theory and Theology," in J. S. Bixler, R. L. Calhoun, and H. R. Niebuhr, eds., *The Nature of Religious Experience* (New York: Harper & Bros., 1937), pp. 93–116.

11. Niebuhr, "Reformation," p. 248.   12. Ibid., p. 249.

13. Niebuhr, *The Kingdom of God in America,* p. 88. Niebuhr acknowledges that these three notes are similar to A. E. Taylor's claim that God, grace and eternal life are characteristic of all advanced religions.

14. Ibid., pp. 51, 124, 193.   15. Ibid., p. 167.

16. Niebuhr, *Meaning of Revelation,* pp. viii–ix.

17. Ibid., p. vii.   18. Ibid., pp. 21–22, italics mine.

19. Ibid., p. 190, italics mine.

Chapter III

1. "An Aspect of the Idea of God in Recent Thought," *Magazin für Evangelische Theologie und Kirche* 48 (1920): 39 ff.; "The Alliance Between Labor and Religion," ibid. 49 (1921): 197 ff.; Christianity and the Social Problem," ibid. 50 (1922); 278 ff.

2. H. Richard Niebuhr, "Back to Benedict," *Christian Century* 42 (1925): 860–61.

3. Niebuhr, *Sources of Denominationalism,* p. 21.

4. Ibid., p. 278.   5. Ibid., pp. 278–79.   6. Ibid., p. 284.

7. "The Grace of Doing Nothing," *Christian Century* 49 (1932): 378–80; "A Communication: The Only Way into the Kingdom of God," ibid., p. 447. Cf. Reinhold Niebuhr's article "Must We Do Nothing?" ibid., pp. 415–17.

8. Niebuhr compared his own discovery to Luther's *Tumerlebnis* or so-called "tower experience." See Sydney E. Ahlstrom, "H. Richard Niebuhr's Place in American Thought," *Christianity and Crisis* 23 (1963): 215.

9. Niebuhr, "Reformation," p. 249.

10. "Constructive Protestantism" is Niebuhr's term for that form of

Christian faith which *dialectically* joins iconoclasm and regeneration, the kingdom of God and the kingdoms of men.

11. Niebuhr, *Kingdom of God*, p. xii.

12. Ibid., pp. xiii–xvi. On pages xv–xvi Niebuhr foreshadows the later argument of *Christ and Culture* in full. While recognizing a variety of strategies and stances on the church-world issue in Christian history, Niebuhr sees their relationship as an unending process of reformation.

13. Though Niebuhr's concern for the reformation of the church was a lifelong concern, from this time on he progressively lost interest in the ecumenical movement as a means or an end for such a renewal.

14. H. Richard Niebuhr, "The Responsibility of the Church for Society," in Kenneth Scott Latourette, ed., *The Gospel, the Church and the World* (New York: Harper & Bros., 1946), pp. 111–33.

15. Ibid., pp. 119–20.   16. Ibid., p. 126, italics mine.

17. Niebuhr, *Christ and Culture*, pp. 45–82, 83–115.

18. Ibid., pp. 116–48.   19. Ibid., pp. 149–89.

20. Ibid., pp. 190–229.

PART TWO

Chapter IV

1. Niebuhr, *Meaning of Revelation*, pp. 74–76.

2. This shift is a response to the secularizing and relativizing of life and thought in the modern world. For a fuller discussion see Chapter XI.

3. Niebuhr, *Meaning of Revelation*, pp. 7–38.

4. Ibid., pp. 9–16; H. Richard Niebuhr, "The Idea of Covenant and American Democracy," *Church History* 23 (1954): 129.

5. Niebuhr, *Meaning of Revelation*, pp. 18–19.

6. Ibid., p. 21; cf. pp. 10–11, 72 ff.; Niebuhr, *Radical Monotheism*, pp. 115 ff.; *Christ and Culture*, p. 238; "The Ego-Alter Dialectic and the Conscience," *Journal of Philosophy* 42 (1945): 354; "The Gift of the Catholic Vision," *Theology Today* 4 (1948): 510 ff.

7. Niebuhr, *Meaning of Revelation*, p. 10.

8. H. Richard Niebuhr, "The Triad of Faith," *Andover Newton Bulletin* 47 (1954): 3–12; "On the Nature of Faith," in Sidney Hook, ed., *Religious Experience and Truth* (New York: New York University Press, 1961), pp. 93–102; *Radical Monotheism*, pp. 16–23.

9. Niebuhr, *Meaning of Revelation*, p. 21.

10. Ibid., pp. 38–42.   11. Ibid., 41–42.

12. Niebuhr, *Christ and Culture*, p. 238.

13. Ibid., p. x. Niebuhr at times also characterized his overall position as "historical relativism" and "historical relationism." But

"theocentric relativism" most clearly expresses both notes of divine sovereignty and human historicity.

14. Niebuhr, *Purpose of the Church*, p. 112.

15. Niebuhr, *Radical Monotheism*, p. 12.

16. Niebuhr, *Meaning of Revelation*, pp. 48–53, 58; cf. "The Doctrine of the Trinity and the Unity of the Church," *Theology Today* 3 (1946): 371–84.

17. Niebuhr, *Meaning of Revelation*, p. 42.

Chapter V

1. Niebuhr, *Meaning of Revelation*, pp. 43–90.

2. Ibid., pp. 59–60, 63, 74–76, 81; *Christ and Culture*, p. x; *Responsible Self*, pp. 45, 69, 79–81, 90–107.

3. Niebuhr, *Meaning of Revelation*, pp. 75–96.

4. Ibid., pp. 66–67.

5. Ibid., pp. 94–99; *Responsible Self*, pp. 79–81, 96, 151–54, 161.

6. Niebuhr, *Meaning of Revelation*, pp. 99–109; *Responsible Self*, pp. 149–60; "The Idea of Covenant and American Democracy," pp. 129–30.

7. Niebuhr, *Meaning of Revelation*, pp. 64, 93–97; *Responsible Self*, p. 79.

8. Niebuhr, *Meaning of Revelation*, pp. 64–66, 97–99, 104–6, 143–47; *Radical Monotheism*, pp. 45–48.

9. Niebuhr, *Meaning of Revelation*, p. 65.

10. Ibid., p. 14; *Purpose of the Church*, p. 22; *Responsible Self*, pp. 79–82, 95–96.

11. Niebuhr, *Meaning of Revelation*, pp. 20–21; *Radical Monotheism*, pp. 115 ff.

12. Niebuhr, "Reformation: Continuing Imperative," p. 249; *Meaning of Revelation*, p. 13; *Responsible Self*, pp. 90–107, 161.

13. Niebuhr, *Meaning of Revelation*, pp. 55–56, 84–86, 89.

14. Niebuhr, *Purpose of the Church*, pp. 120–23; *Meaning of Revelation*, pp. 63, 84–90.

15. Niebuhr, *Meaning of Revelation*, pp. 59–63, 67–73, 86–88, 91–93, 125–28; cf. *Responsible Self*, pp. 175–78.

16. Niebuhr, *Meaning of Revelation*, p. 42.

17. Ibid., pp. 68–72, 110–31; *Responsible Self*, pp. 69–107.

18. Niebuhr, *Meaning of Revelation*, p. 69; cf., pp. 13, 110–31.

19. Ibid., pp. 7–22, 70–71, 110–31; *Christ and Culture*, pp. 241–49; *Responsible Self*, pp. 71–72, 77–78.

20. Niebuhr, *Meaning of Revelation*, pp. 89–90; *Purpose of the Church*, pp. 43–44, 86–87.

21. Niebuhr, *Meaning of Revelation*, pp. 89–90; cf., pp. 50–51, 71,

148; *Purpose of the Church*, pp. 43–44, 86–87, 119–20; *Christ and Culture*, pp. 12–13.

22. Niebuhr, *Meaning of Revelation*, p. 31.

23. H. Richard Niebuhr, "Issues Between Protestants and Catholics," *Religion in Life* 23 (1954): 203; *Meaning of Revelation*, pp. vii–ix; *Purpose of the Church*, p. 25.

24. Niebuhr, *Purpose of the Church*, pp. 88–89, 120.

25. Niebuhr, *Christ and Culture*, pp. 12–13; *Purpose of the Church*, p. 30.

26. H. Richard Niebuhr, "The Norm of the Church," *Journal of Religious Thought* 4 (1946): 8–15; "The Gift of the Catholic Vision," pp. 507–521; *Meaning of Revelation*, pp. 20–21; *Christ and Culture*, pp. 231–56.

27. Niebuhr, "Evangelical and Protestant Ethics," p. 212.

Chapter VI

1. Niebuhr, *Meaning of Revelation*, pp. 50–51, 71, 89–90; *Purpose of the Church*, pp. 43–44, 119–20.

2. Niebuhr, *Meaning of Revelation*, pp. 109–110; *Responsible Self*, pp. 154–59. Especially see Niebuhr's three articles on war: "War as the Judgment of God," pp. 630–33; "Is God in the War?" pp. 953–55; "War as Crucifixion," pp. 513–15.

3. Niebuhr, *Meaning of Revelation*, pp. 46–48, 138–41, 148–49; *Christ and Culture*, pp. 254–55; *Radical Monotheism*, pp. 42–44, 124–25; *Responsible Self*, pp. 143–44, 155–56, 177–78.

4. Niebuhr, "Evangelical and Protestant Ethics," p. 222.

5. Niebuhr, *Radical Monotheism*, p. 117.

6. H. Richard Niebuhr, "Life is Worth Living," *Intercollegian and Far Horizons* 57 (1939): 4.

7. Niebuhr, *Meaning of Revelation*, p. 77.

8. Niebuhr, "On the Nature of Faith," pp. 93–102.

9. Ibid., p. 100.

10. Ibid.; *Radical Monotheism*, pp. 16 ff.; *Christ and Culture*, pp. 252 ff.; *Responsible Self*, pp. 83–89.

11. Niebuhr, *Radical Monotheism*, pp. 16–23, 110–11, 118; *Responsible Self*, pp. 119–21.

12. Niebuhr, "The Triad of Faith," p. 8; "On the Nature of Faith," pp. 93–102; *Radical Monotheism*, pp. 16–23; *Responsible Self*, pp. 79, 118–21.

13. Niebuhr, *Radical Monotheism*, pp. 24–37; *Meaning of Revelation*, pp. 94–104; *Responsible Self*, pp. 108–126.

14. Niebuhr, *Radical Monotheism*, p. 119.   15. Ibid., p. 120.

16. Niebuhr, *Meaning of Revelation*, pp. 77–78; *Radical Monotheism*, pp. 24–31; *Responsible Self*, pp. 98–100, 106, 121–23, 137–40;

"Man the Sinner," *Journal of Religion* 15 (1935): 278–80; "Life Is Worth Living," p. 4; *Church Against the World*, pp. 123–38.

17. Niebuhr, *Radical Monotheism*, pp. 25–31; "Man the Sinner," pp. 278–79.

18. Niebuhr, *Radical Monotheism*, pp. 35–37, 56–60, 75–76; *Responsible Self*, pp. 140–41.

19. Niebuhr, *Radical Monotheism*, pp. 122–23; *Responsible Self*, pp. 139–41.

20. Niebuhr, *Radical Monotheism*, pp. 123–24.

21. Niebuhr, *Responsible Self*, pp. 142–45.

22. Niebuhr, "Man the Sinner," p. 279; *Radical Monotheism*, pp. 124–26; *Responsible Self*, pp. 143–44, 175–76.

23. Niebuhr, "Reformation: Continuing Imperative," p. 249, italics mine. Cf. *Responsible Self*, pp. 143–45, 174–78; *Radical Monotheism*, pp. 43–44, 59, 124–25; "The Triad of Faith," pp. 9–10; *Meaning of Revelation*, p. 154.

24. Niebuhr, *Purpose of the Church*, p. 34.

25. Niebuhr expresses his "prosopic" approach as a "moral description" in *Christ and Culture* and in terms of the root metaphor of "responsibility" in *Responsible Self*. But in each case he acknowledges the helpfulness of other approaches to the "essence" of Jesus Christ, e.g., metaphysical and historical (*Christ and Culture*, pp. 14, 29) or deontological and teleological (*Responsible Self*, pp. 136, 160–63).

26. Niebuhr, *Radical Monotheism*, pp. 40, 44–48; *Meaning of Revelation*, pp. 109–137; *Christ and Culture*, pp. 191–96.

27. Niebuhr, *Christ and Culture*, pp. 15–29; *Responsible Self*, p. 144.

28. Niebuhr, *Radical Monotheism*, p. 42.

29. Niebuhr, *Christ and Culture*, pp. 14–29, 254–55; "The Triad of Faith," pp. 9–10; *Responsible Self*, pp. 165–67.

30. Niebuhr, "The Doctrine of the Trinity and the Unity of the Church," pp. 374–76.

31. Niebuhr, "Reformation: Continuing Imperative," p. 250; *Purpose of the Church*, pp. 31, 45–46; *Radical Monotheism*, pp. 57–60; *Responsible Self*, p. 86.

32. Niebuhr, *Purpose of the Church*, pp. 31, 45; *Meaning of Revelation*, 183–85.

33. Niebuhr, *Radical Monotheism*, pp. 57–60; *Responsible Self*, p. 172; "Reformation: Continuing Imperative," p. 250.

34. Niebuhr, *Meaning of Revelation*, pp. viii–ix.

35. Niebuhr, "The Triad of Faith," p. 10.

36. Niebuhr, *Responsible Self*, pp. 108–126, 161–78; cf. D. M. Baillie's "paradox of grace" in *God Was in Christ* (New York: Charles Scribner's Sons, 1948), pp. 114–32.

37. Niebuhr, *Meaning of Revelation*, p. 166; *Christ and Culture*, pp.

254–55; *Radical Monotheism,* pp. 123–24; *Responsible Self,* pp. 176–77; "The Triad of Faith," p. 10.

38. Niebuhr, *Responsible Self,* pp. 176–77. Cf. *Christ and Culture,* p. 254; "Reformation: Continuing Imperative," p. 249. Niebuhr speaks of this coming to faith as a "surd" or a "miracle." He does not mean that this experience *contradicts* natural processes and scientific explanations but that the experiences cannot be *reduced* to these dynamics.

39. Niebuhr, *Kingdom of God in America,* pp. 115–16; *Christ and Culture,* p. 254; *Radical Monotheism,* pp. 50, 124–25; *Responsible Self,* pp. 176–77.

40. "War as Crucifixion," pp. 514, 515.

41. Niebuhr, *Meaning of Revelation,* pp. 130–31, 149–50; *Christ and Culture,* p. 255; *Responsible Self,* pp. 112–15.

42. Niebuhr, *Christ and Culture,* p. 255; *Responsible Self,* p. 177.

43. Niebuhr, *Christ and Culture,* p. 13; *Responsible Self,* p. 176; "The Norm of the Church," p. 13.

44. Compare Niebuhr's fragmentary account to the further developed and similar position of his son, Richard R. Niebuhr, *Resurrection and Historical Reason* (New York: Charles Scribner's Sons, 1957).

45. Niebuhr, *Christ and Culture,* p. 194. Cf. "The Triad of Faith," pp. 11–12; "Man the Sinner," p. 273, "Reformation: Continuing Imperative," p. 248; *Christ and Culture,* pp. 193–94.

46. Niebuhr, *Meaning of Revelation,* pp. viii, 155–91; *Purpose of the Church,* pp. 36–37; "Value Theory and Theology," p. 116.

47. Niebuhr, *Meaning of Revelation,* pp. 151–91. Cf. *Radical Monotheism,* pp. 46–48.

48. Niebuhr, *Meaning of Revelation,* pp. 86–87.

49. Ibid., pp. 125–30.

50. Ibid., p. 129. Cf. *Christ and Culture,* p. 255; *Responsible Self,* pp. 154–57, 175–78.

51. Niebuhr, *Meaning of Revelation,* p. 109; *Responsible Self,* pp. 102–7, 120.

52. Niebuhr, *Meaning of Revelation,* p. 175; *Radical Monotheism,* pp. 78–89, 93–99, 127–41.

53. Niebuhr, *Meaning of Revelation,* pp. 109–137; *Radical Monotheism,* pp. 47–48; *Responsible Self,* pp. 95–107, 121–26.

54. Niebuhr, *Meaning of Revelation,* pp. 99–109, 118–20; *Responsible Self,* pp. 121–22, 125–26, 137–39.

55. Niebuhr, *Meaning of Revelation,* pp. 118–31; *Responsible Self,* pp. 122–23, 175–78.

56. Niebuhr, *Meaning of Revelation,* p. 137.

57. I first suggested the tetrahedron as a more appropriate model than a triangle in my doctoral dissertation, "Christology and Methodology in H. Richard Niebuhr" (Ph.D. diss., Duke University, 1963).

Recently James W. Fowler has shown how fruitful this image is for "visualizing" the complexity of Niebuhr's thought. See Fowler, *To See the Kingdom*, pp. 165–66, 182–84, 198–200.

PART THREE

Chapter VII

1. Niebuhr, *Responsible Self*, p. 48.

2. See Joseph Fletcher, *Moral Responsibility* (Philadelphia: The Westminster Press, 1967); Thomas W. Ogletree, "From Anxiety to Responsibility," *The Chicago Theological Seminary Register* 43 (1968); Kenneth Boulding, "The Principle of Personal Responsibility," *Beyond Economics* (Ann Arbor: The University of Michigan Press, 1968); Robert O. Johann, S. J., "Authority and Responsibility," *Freedom and Man*, ed. John Courtney, S. J. (New York: P. J. Kenedy and Sons, 1965); Herbert Fingarette, *On Responsibility* (New York: Basic Books, 1967); Albert R. Jonson, *Responsibility in Modern Religious Ethics* (Washington, D.C.: Corpus Books, 1968); Eric Mount, Jr., *Conscience and Responsibility* (Richmond: John Knox Press, 1969); C. Freeman Sleeper, *Black Power and Christian Responsibility* (Nashville: Abingdon Press, 1969); James Gustafson, "Christian Ethics and Social Policy," pp. 119–39 in *Faith and Ethics*, ed. Paul Ramsey; Waldo Beach, "A Theological Analysis of Race Relations," ibid., pp. 205–224.

3. Niebuhr, *Responsible Self*, pp. 45–46.

4. Niebuhr, *Sources of Denominationalism*, p. 274. The phrase "the responsible self" first appears in *Church Against the World*, p. 4.

5. Niebuhr, *Responsible Self*, pp. 47–68.   6. Ibid., pp. 55–60.

7. Niebuhr was influenced in this regard by Stephen Pepper's "root metaphor" theory of metaphysical reflection and Ernst Cassirer's philosophy of "symbolic forms." See Stephen Pepper, *World Hypotheses* (Berkeley: University of California Press, 1961) and Ernst Cassirer, *An Essay on Man* (Garden City: Doubleday Anchor Books, 1953).

8. Niebuhr, *Responsible Self*, pp. 48–54.

9. Ibid., p. 56.   10. Ibid., pp. 56–61.   11. Ibid., p. 56.

12. Ibid., pp. 56–60.   13. Ibid., pp. 65–67.

14. Ibid., p. 65.   15. Ibid., pp. 60–61.

16. Niebuhr, "The Responsibility of the Church for Society," pp. 113–20.

17. Ibid., pp. 114–15.   18. Niebuhr, *Responsible Self*, p. 65.

19. Ibid., pp. 69–89.   20. Ibid., pp. 61–63.

21. Niebuhr, *Meaning of Revelation*, p. 108.

22. Niebuhr, *Responsible Self*, pp. 61, 149–60, 161–78. See his articles on war for examples of this "imagistic" reasoning. "War as the Judgment of God," "Is God in the War?" and "War as Crucifixion."

23. Niebuhr, *Responsible Self*, p. 63.   24. Ibid., pp. 63–65.

25. Ibid., p. 64.   26. Ibid., pp. 65, 69–89.   27. Ibid., p. 83.

28. Niebuhr, *Radical Monotheism*, p. 109; "Value Theory and Theology," p. 106; "Evangelical and Protestant Ethics," p. 223.

29. H. Richard Niebuhr, "The Hidden Church and the Churches in Sight," *Religion in Life* 15 (1945–46) : 115; "Man the Sinner," p. 278; *Meaning of Revelation*, p. 77; *Radical Monotheism*, pp. 24–30.

30. Niebuhr, *Responsible Self*, p. 119.

31. Ibid., pp. 109, 112, 115.   32. Ibid., pp. 140–43.

33. Niebuhr, "Evangelical and Protestant Ethics," p. 223.

34. Niebuhr, *Responsible Self*, pp. 143–44.

35. Niebuhr, *Radical Monotheism*, p. 31.

36. Niebuhr, *Responsible Self*, pp. 142–43.

37. Ibid., pp. 139, 120.

38. Ibid., p. 144. Cf. *Radical Monotheism*, p. 125.

39. Niebuhr, *Radical Monotheism*, p. 124; *Responsible Self*, pp. 119–21.

40. Niebuhr, *Responsible Self*, pp. 144–45.

41. Ibid., pp. 161–78.

Chapter VIII

1. Niebuhr, "Evangelical and Protestant Ethics," p. 220; *Radical Monotheism*, pp. 31–37, 112–13; "Responsibility of the Church for Society," pp. 117–18.

2. Niebuhr, "Evangelical and Protestant Ethics," pp. 220–22; *Radical Monotheism*, pp. 49–63.

3. Niebuhr, *Radical Monotheism*, p. 33.   4. Ibid., pp. 44–48.

5. Niebuhr, *Responsible Self*, p. 126.

6. Niebuhr, "The Center of Value," pp. 100–113.

7. Niebuhr, *Radical Monotheism*, p. 38; cf. pp. 108–9.

8. Niebuhr, *Responsible Self*, pp. 86–89, 171–72; "'The Responsibility of the Church for Society," pp. 119–20.

9. Niebuhr, *Responsible Self*, pp. 123–24, italics mine.

10. Niebuhr, *Radical Monotheism*, pp. 34–37, 126; *Responsible Self*, p. 83; *Purpose of the Church*, pp. 37–39; *Meaning of Revelation*, pp. 166–67.

11. Niebuhr, *Purpose of the Church*, p. 38.

12. Niebuhr, *Responsible Self*, pp. 107–9.

13. Niebuhr, *Radical Monotheism*, pp. 100–113.

14. Niebuhr, *Purpose of the Church*, pp. 37–39.

15. Niebuhr, *Radical Monotheism*, p. 37.

16. Niebuhr, *Responsible Self*, pp. 60–61. To parallel the Greek titles for the other great symbols of the moral life (*teleological* and *deonto-*

logical), Niebuhr sometimes referred to response ethics as *cathēkontic* ethics, or the ethics of the fitting. Ibid., p. 87.

17. Ibid., p. 97. By *verifact* Niebuhr means a verified scientific theory or claim. He uses the term to focus attention on the context-dependent character of even scientific beliefs.

18. See Niebuhr, *Meaning of Revelation,* pp. 186–87; *Responsible Self,* pp. 162–73; *Christ and Culture,* pp. 11–29.

19. The discussion that follows is based on lecture notes from Niebuhr's course "Christian Ethics" transcribed by Robert Yetter, Gene Canestrari, and Ed Elliott in 1952. Pagination is from my typescript which does not correspond to the pagination of the mimeographed original.

20. Niebuhr, "Christian Ethics," pp. 132–47.

21. Ibid., p. 147.   22. Ibid., pp. 147–67.

23. Niebuhr, "Toward the Emancipation of the Church," p. 144; "War as Crucifixion," pp. 514–15; "War as the Judgment of God," p. 631; *Church Against the World,* p. 154; *Meaning of Revelation,* pp. 186–87; *Radical Monotheism,* p. 125.

24. Niebuhr, "Christian Ethics," pp. 160–67.

25. Niebuhr, "Man the Sinner," p. 280.

26. Niebuhr, *Church Against the World,* p. 12, italics mine.

27. Rexford F. Tucker, "H. Richard Niebuhr and the Ethics of Responsibility" (Ph.D. diss., Drew University, 1970), p. 164.

28. Niebuhr, "Value Theory and Theology," p. 116.

29. Niebuhr, *Meaning of Revelation,* pp. 175–91.

30. Niebuhr, "The Grace of Doing Nothing," pp. 358–60; "A Communication: The Only Way into the Kingdom of God," p. 447.

31. Niebuhr has no major section on race relations in his ethics lectures because he does not regard racial or ethnic groupings as legitimate communities of the common life. But this exclusion of racism as a special area of problems in the common life expresses his antipathy to all racism. "Christian Ethics," pp. 179.

Chapter IX

1. Niebuhr, *Radical Monotheism,* pp. 49–99.
2. Ibid., pp 49–63.
3. Niebuhr, "Reformation: Continuing Imperative," p. 249.
4. Niebuhr, "Christian Ethics," pp. 179–82.
5. Niebuhr, *Purpose of the Church,* pp. 19–27.
6. Ibid., p. 20.   7. Ibid., pp. 23–24.   8. Ibid., p. 26.
9. Niebuhr, "The Responsibility of the Church for Society."
10. For example, see "The Grace of Doing Nothing." For Niebuhr's critique of communism, see "The Irreligion of Communist and Capitalist," *The Christian Century* 47 (1930): 1306–7.

11. Niebuhr, "The Responsibility of the Church for Society," pp. 126–32.

12. Ibid., p. 129.   13. Ibid., p. 130.   14. Ibid., p. 142.

PART FOUR

Chapter X

1. For Niebuhr's clearest statements on God as "the structure of reality" see "War as the Judgment of God"; "The Grace of Doing Nothing"; "The Only Way into the Kingdom"; *Christ and Culture,* pp. 236, 249–56; *Responsible Self,* pp. 109–126.

2. See John B. Cobb, *God and the World* (Philadelphia: Westminster Press, 1969), pp. 87–102.

3. Niebuhr, *Meaning of Revelation,* p. 187.   4. Ibid., p. ix.

Chapter XI

1. The best detailed analysis of the contemporary context of theological reflection is Langdon Gilkey, *Naming the Whirlwind: The Renewal of God-Language* (Indianapolis and New York: The Bobbs-Merrill Co., 1969), pp. 3–230. For a summary sketch see my *Radical Christianity: The New Theologies in Perspective,* with John Hayes (Anderson, S.C.: Droke House, 1968), pp. 17–44.

2. For a good account, see Andrew M. Greeley, *Unsecular Man: The Persistence of Religion* (New York: Delta Books, 1972).

3. For examples of these new conceptions of divine immanence, see John A. T. Robinson, *Honest to God* (Philadelphia: Westminster Press, 1963); Peter Berger, *A Rumor of Angels* (Garden City: Doubleday and Co., 1969).

4. This term is Otto Muck's who surveys this tradition in *The Transcendental Method* (New York: Herder and Herder, 1968). See for example Karl Rahner, *Spirit in the World* (New York: Herder and Herder, 1968); Bernard Lonergan, *Insight: A Study of Human Understanding* (London: Longmans, Green, 1957).

5. This phrase is furnished by John B. Cobb, *A Christian Natural Theology* (Philadelphia: The Westminster Press, 1965). For other representative statements see Frank B. Dilley, *Metaphysics and Religious Language* (New York: Columbia University Press, 1964); Langdon Gilkey, *Naming the Whirlwind;* Gregory Baum, *Man Becoming* (New York: Herder and Herder, 1970).

6. Niebuhr, *Responsible Self,* p. 45. Significantly, Niebuhr describes his approach in this book as "Christian moral philosophy." "My concern here is with the understanding of human life from a Christian point of view and neither with the understanding of Christian life from some other point of view (such as that of social adjustment or adapta-

tion to nature) nor with the understanding of Christian life only, from a Christian point of view." Ibid., p. 45.

7. For their generic discussions of religion, see Friedrich Schleiermacher, *On Religion* (1799; reprint ed., New York: Harper and Bros. Torchbook, 1958); Paul Tillich, *Dynamics of Faith* (New York: Harper and Bros. Torchbooks, 1958).

8. For a useful survey of language analysis in recent philosophy and theology, see Frederick Ferré, *Language, Logic and God* (New York: Harper & Row, 1961).

9. For example, see Ian G. Barbour, *Issues in Science and Religion* (Englewood Cliffs: Prentice-Hall, Inc., 1966); Frederick Ferré, *Basic Modern Philosophy of Religion* (New York: Charles Scribner's Sons, 1967).

10. For example see Philip Wheelwright, *Metaphor and Reality* (Bloomington: Indiana University Press, 1971): Rollo May, ed., *Symbolism in Religion and Literature* (New York: George Braziller, 1960).

11. For example see James B. Wiggins, ed., *Religion as Story* (New York: Harper & Row, 1975); Wesley A. Kort, *Narrative Elements and Religious Meanings* (Philadelphia: Fortress Press, 1975); James Wm. McClendon, Jr., *Biography as Theology* (Nashville: Abingdon Press, 1974); Sallie TeSelle, *Speaking in Parables* (Philadelphia: Fortress Press, 1975).

12. *Meaning of Revelation*, p. 43. This entire book is a manifesto in personal transformation and world-building through storytelling.

13. See Barry Commoner, *The Closing Circle: Nature, Man and Technology* (New York: Bantam Books, 1972); Frederick Ferré, *Shaping the Future* (New York: Harper & Row, 1976).

14. This connection was first made by a historian addressing the American Academy of Science in 1966. Lyn White, Jr., "The Historical Roots of our Ecologic Crisis," later published in *Science* 155 (1967): 1203-7.

15. See Ian G. Barbour, *Earth Might Be Fair: Reflections on Ethics, Religion and Ecology* (Englewood Cliffs: Prentice-Hall Inc., 1972); John B. Cobb, Jr., *Is It Too Late? A Theology of Ecology* (Beverly Hills: Bruce, 1972).

16. Niebuhr, *Responsible Self*, pp. 123-24; cf. *Meaning of Revelation*, p. 167.

17. Niebuhr, "Reformation: Continuing Imperative," p. 251.

Selected Bibliography

PRINCIPAL WORKS OF H. RICHARD NIEBUHR

The Advancement of Theological Education. With D. D. Williams and J. M. Gustafson. New York: Harper & Bros., 1957.

Christian Ethics: Sources of the Living Tradition. Edited and introduced with Waldo Beach. New York: Ronald Press, 1955. Chapters 1, 8, 9 and 13 by Niebuhr.

The Church Against the World. With Wilhelm Pauck and Francis P. Miller. Chicago: Willett, Clark & Co. 1935. "The Question of the Church," pp. 1–13; "Toward the Independence of the Church," pp. 123–56, by Niebuhr.

Christ and Culture. New York: Harper & Bros., 1951.

The Kingdom of God in America. 1937. Reprint. New York: Harper & Bros., Torchbooks, 1959.

The Meaning of Revelation. New York: The Macmillan Co., 1941.

The Ministry in Historical Perspectives. Edited with D. D. Williams. New York: Harper & Bros., 1956.

The Purpose of the Church and Its Ministry. New York: Harper & Bros., 1956.

Radical Monotheism and Western Culture. New York: Harper & Bros., 1960.

The Responsible Self. New York: Harper & Row, 1963.

The Social Sources of Denominationalism. 1929. Reprint. New York: Meridian Books, 1957.

"The Center of Value." In R. N. Anshen, ed. *Moral Principles of Action*. New York: Harper & Bros., 1952, pp. 162–75.

"The Disorder of Man in the Church of God." In *Man's Disorder and God's Design*. The Amsterdam Assembly Series, vol. 1. New York: Harper & Bros., 1949, pp. 78–88.

"Evangelical and Protestant Ethics." In J. F. Arndt, ed. *The Heritage of the Reformation*. New York: Richard R. Smith, 1950, pp. 211–29.

"How My Mind has Changed." In H. E. Fey, ed. *How My Mind Has Changed*. Cleveland: World Publishing Co., Meridian Books, 1961, pp. 69–80.

"On the Nature of Faith." In Sidney Hook, ed. *Religious Experience and Truth*. New York: New York University Press, 1961, pp. 93–102.

"The Protestant Movement and Democracy in the United States." In James Ward Smith and A. Leland Jamison, eds. *The Shaping of American Religion*. Princeton: Princeton University Press, 1961, pp. 20–71.

"Religious Realism in the Twentieth Century." In D. C. Macintosh, ed. *Religious Realism*. New York: The Macmillan Co., 1931, pp. 413–28.

"The Responsibility of the Church for Society." In K. S. Latourette, ed. *The Gospel, the Church and the World*. New York: Harper & Bros., 1946, pp. 111–33.

"Soren Kierkegaard." In Carl Michalson, ed. *Christianity and the Existentialists*. New York: Charles Scribner's Sons, 1956, pp. 23–42.

"Value Theory and Theology." In *The Nature of Religious Experience, Essays in Honor of D. C. Macintosh*. New York: Harper & Bros., 1937, pp. 93–116.

BOOKS ABOUT H. RICHARD NIEBUHR

Cobb, John B. *Living Options in Protestant Theology*. Philadelphia: Westminster Press, 1962, pp. 284–301.

Fowler, James W. *To See the Kingdom*. Nashville: Abingdon Press, 1974.

Godsey, John D. *The Promise of H. Richard Niebuhr*. Philadelphia: J. B. Lippincott Co., 1970.

Hoedemaker, L. A. *The Theology of H. Richard Niebuhr*. Philadelphia: Pilgrim Press, 1970.

Holbrook, Clyde A. "H. Richard Niebuhr." In *A Handbook of Christian Theologians*. Edited by Martin E. Marty and Dean G. Peerman. Cleveland and New York: The World Publishing Co., 1965, pp. 375–95.

Ramsey, Paul, ed. *Faith and Ethics: The Theology of H. Richard Niebuhr*. New York: Harper & Bros., 1957.

Ramsey, Paul. *Nine Modern Moralists.* Englewood Cliffs, N.J.: Prentice-Hall, Inc., 1962, pp. 149–179.

Soper, David Wesley. *Major Voices in American Theology.* Philadelphia: The Westminster Press, 1953, pp. 153–90.

Thelan, Mary Francis. *Man as Sinner in Contemporary American Realistic Theology.* New York: Kings Crown Press, 1946, pp. 148–163.

Fuller bibliographies of primary and secondary source materials may be found in Ramsey, *Faith and Ethics* and Fowler, *To See the Kingdom.*